## About Island Press

Island Press is the only nonprofit organization in the United States whose principal purpose is the publication of books on environmental issues and natural resource management. We provide solutions-oriented information to professionals, public officials, business and community leaders, and concerned citizens who are shaping responses to environmental problems.

In 1994, Island Press celebrated its tenth anniversary as the leading provider of timely and practical books that take a multidisciplinary approach to critical environmental concerns. Our growing list of titles reflects our commitment to bringing the best of an expanding body of literature to the environmental community throughout North America and the world.

Support for Island Press is provided by Apple Computer, Inc., The Bullitt Foundation, The Geraldine R. Dodge Foundation, The Energy Foundation, The Ford Foundation, The W. Alton Jones Foundation, The Lyndhurst Foundation, The John D. and Catherine T. MacArthur Foundation, The Andrew W. Mellon Foundation, The Joyce Mertz-Gilmore Foundation, The National Fish and Wildlife Foundation, The Pew Charitable Trusts, The Pew Global Stewardship Initiative, The Rockefeller Philanthropic Collaborative, Inc., and individual donors.

## About The Conservation Fund

The Conservation Fund is a national nonprofit organization that protects land and water through partnerships with corporations, nonprofit organizations, and public agencies. Since 1986, The Conservation Fund has acquired and protected more than 1,300,000 acres of land valued at nearly $590 million for only $206 million. The Conservation Fund helps gateway communities and public agencies protect land resources, including wetlands, wildlife refuges, abandoned rail corridors, historic and battlefield sites, scenic areas, greenways, and other areas of natural or cultural significance. In addition to land conservation activities, the Fund has an American Greenways program that assists in the development of greenways and trails; a Civil War Battlefield campaign to safeguard America's Civil War battlefield sites; a Freshwater Institute to develop economically feasible and environmentally sound approaches to use of freshwater resources; and a Land Advisory Service to provide sound land-use planning, ecological assessment, and technical assistance on land conservation and development.

## About the Sonoran Institute

The Sonoran Institute is a nonprofit organization based in Tucson, Arizona, dedicated to promoting community-based strategies that preserve the ecological integrity of protected lands, and at the same time meeting the economic aspirations of adjoining landowners and communities. Underlying the Institute's mission is the conviction that community-driven and inclusive approaches to conservation produce the most effective results. The Sonoran Institute is committed to testing a wide range of approaches to community-based conservation, and adapting these approaches based on real experiences. The Institute also is committed to widely disseminating both its findings and the tools it develops. The Institute operates in the western U.S. and northwestern Mexico, and works primarily with communities adjacent to protected areas and public lands with significant natural values.

# Balancing
# Nature and Commerce
# in Gateway Communities

# Balancing
# Nature and Commerce
# in Gateway Communities

Jim Howe, Ed McMahon, and Luther Propst

THE CONSERVATION FUND AND THE SONORAN INSTITUTE

**ISLAND PRESS**
Washington, D.C. ■ Covelo, California

This publication was made possible through the generous support of the Ittleson Foundation, National Fish and Wildlife Foundation, National Park Foundation, and Henry P. Kendall Foundation.

Cover and frontispiece: An early morning moonset over Red Lodge, Montana. A gateway to the Yellowstone ecosystem, Red Lodge demonstrates what a community can do when residents play an active role in determining their future. See the case study on page 113 for more details. (Photo by Merv Coleman)

Library of Congress Cataloging-in-Publication Data

Howe, Jim, 1961–
    Balancing nature and commerce in gateway communities/Jim Howe
  Ed McMahon, Luther Propst.
      p.    cm.
    Includes bibliographical references and index.
    ISBN 1-55963-545-2
    1. Land use, Rural—Environmental aspects—United States. 2. Land
  use, Rural—Economic aspects—United States. 3. Real estate
  development—Environmental aspects—United States. 4. Biotic
  communities—Economic aspects—United States. 5. Community
  development—Environmental aspects—United States. 6. Nature
  conservation—Economic aspects—United States—Case studies.
  I. McMahon, Edward, 1947–    .   II. Propst, Luther.   III. Title.
  HD256.H77   1997
  333.76´15´0973—dc21                                        97-19642
                                                                CIP

Printed on recycled, acid-free paper ♻

Manufactured in the United States of America

10  9  8  7  6  5  4  3  2

# Contents

# Acknowledgments

Many people have contributed to this effort and provided valuable insights about the issues and solutions described in the book. We want to especially recognize and express our gratitude to Chris Duerksen. While a senior associate at The Conservation Foundation, Chris's research into the factors that correlate with effective local growth management provided the framework and many of the core ideas for this book. This book would not have been written but for his initiative.

Other colleagues who helped conceptualize these materials include Michael Mantell and Doug Wheeler, formerly of World Wildlife Fund and The Conservation Foundation. Economist Ray Rasker of The Wilderness Society also was instrumental in the chapters on the economic value of quality of life and tourism.

Many others provided valuable comments or contributions. They include Fred Bosselman, Mike Boylan, Don Briggs, Mark Briggs, David J. Brower, Gordon Brown, Warren Brown, Dan Carol, Bill Chandler, John Clayton, Bill Collins, Peyton Curlee, Tom DePaolo, Lill Erickson, Gary Ferguson, Denny Galvin, Larry Gamble, Catherine Gilliam, Jan Gingold, Dennis Glick, Frank Gregg, Bill Hedden, Elizabeth Humstone, Michael Kinsley, Lenora Kirby, Jake Kittle, Gil Lusk, Mark Muro, Gary Nabhan, Lee Nellis, Pat Noonan, Ken Olson, Bill Paleck, Jim Pissot, Tom Power, Ben and Anne Read, Liz Rosan, Andy Ruff, Mary Schmid, John Shepard, Sandy Shuptrine, Dave Simon, Gary Stolz, Roger Stone, Bill Towler, Alan Turnbull, Bill Walters,

Elizabeth Watson, and Brooke Williams. Larry Howe deserves special mention for his expertise in editing and wordsmithing.

Each of the profiles and case studies was compiled through interviews with members of the local community: elected officials, land-use planners, developers, and farmers and ranchers. All these people have earned our admiration and respect for the inspiring work they are doing to demonstrate sound, local land-use and economic development policies. Indeed, this book could not have been written without them.

We also are indebted to several photographers, especially to Robert Glenn Ketchum, both for his outstanding photographs and for his inspiring instruction in the value of combining art with advocacy. We also thank Merv Coleman for the stunning photograph of Red Lodge, Montana, on the cover.

At the Sonoran Institute, we want to thank Yoly Ostertag and Dawn Willman for their administrative support and patience and Liz Rosan for her able assistance in compiling photographs and materials. At The Conservation Fund, we wish to thank Jody Tick, Jack Lynn, and Liz Madison for their support and guidance.

It has also been a pleasure to work with Heather Boyer at Island Press, who had the difficult task of convincing us what is necessary to publish this work.

A final word of gratitude is due the National Park Foundation, the National Fish and Wildlife Foundation, and the Ittleson Foundation, whose financial support enabled the research and writing of this book. In particular, we express our thanks to Wilke Nelson, Whitney Tilt, Jonathan Davis, and Tony Wood for their patience and intellectual contributions to the concept and later the manuscript. We also acknowledge the William and Flora Hewlett Foundation, the Henry P. Kendall Foundation, and the Richard King Mellon Foundation.

Finally, Jim, Ed, and Luther are deeply grateful to their families and friends for their support. Luther and Ed also want to express gratitude to their wives for their patience with seemingly never-ending travel schedules.

Chapter 1

# Introduction

Since the 1950s, Americans have been migrating from urban areas of the United States to its rapidly growing suburbs. In our quest for the American dream, we flocked to places like Tysons Corner, Virginia; the San Fernando Valley, California; Aurora, Colorado; and Federal Way, Washington.

Today, these suburbs reveal the downside of 40 years of poorly managed growth: Communities that once promised refuge from the ills of the city have been transformed into congested towns with clogged highways, burgeoning crime rates, and mile after mile of look-alike shopping malls, franchise architecture, and soulless housing tracts.

It should come as no surprise, then, that Americans are once again on the move, this time in a migration that pushes growth even farther into the countryside. Increasing numbers of people are fleeing the suburbs and choosing to live in the small towns and open spaces surrounding America's magnificent national and state parks, wildlife refuges, forests, historic sites, wilderness areas, and other public lands.

*Gateway communities*—the towns and cities that border these public lands—are the destinations of choice for much of the country's migrating populace. With their scenic beauty and high quality of life, gateway communities have become a magnet for millions of Americans looking to escape the congestion, banality, and faster tempo of life in the suburbs and cities.

*Increasing numbers of Americans are choosing to live next to national parks, national wildlife refuges, and other public lands and natural areas. For the communities around them, the result is change, often at an unprecedented pace. (Dan Dagget)*

Estes Park, Colorado, gateway to Rocky Mountain National Park, and St. George, Utah, gateway to Zion National Park, have become havens for retirees looking for a picturesque place to spend their golden years. During the 1980s, the population of Estes Park grew by more than 35 percent; St. George's population doubled.

People who want to live close to recreational opportunities are inundating Maryville, Tennessee, and other communities adjoining Great Smoky Mountains National Park. "East Tennessee has just exploded," says Randy Brown, a Maryville resident, "and the people moving here all want to live near the park."

Thousands of discontented city dwellers from the East and West Coasts are selling their homes and using the profits to relocate to gateway communities with lower costs of living. Termed *equity exiles*, many of these urban refugees are facing the same congestion and problems they thought they were leaving behind. Traverse City, Michigan; Prescott, Arizona; and Durango, Colorado, are just a few of the gateway communities that are now struggling to cope with growth-related problems. Whatever the reasons behind it, this new wave of migration shows no signs of abating. If current demographic trends continue, gateway communities will experience astronomical growth rates for at least the next 20 years.

Americans have always wanted to spend their leisure time removed from the pressures of their daily lives. Today, they have the financial resources to do so. Sociologists attribute a rising demand for second homes and resort vacations in pristine and scenic areas to the aging of the baby-boom generation. Over the next decade, there will be a 50 percent increase in the number of Americans in the 45–54 age bracket, a group with a significant amount of disposable income and leisure time.

What's more, according to a recent study by economists at Cornell University, baby boomers stand to inherit some $10.4 trillion in stock market gains and real estate assets salted away by their parents. Armed with this inheritance, boomers are expected to double the demand for recreational homes and resort lodging in gateway communities.

## Changes Ahead

Unlike many U.S. cities and suburbs, gateway communities offer what an increasing number of Americans value: a clean environment, safe streets, and a friendly, small-town atmosphere. But just as in the suburbs, unplanned growth and rapid development in gateway communities can create the same social and scenic ills from which many Americans are now fleeing. Worse, rising real estate values and higher property taxes brought on by an increased demand for housing can force lifelong residents from the communities they call home. Skyrocketing property values can quickly translate into housing shortages for longtime residents.

In Bozeman, Montana, for example, a gateway to Yellowstone National Park, the demand for housing and real estate has dramatically affected property values. In 1981, the average cost of a suburban acre near Bozeman was $600; in 1994, that same acre brought as much as $10,000.

In Tremont, Maine, surging demand for land and housing has displaced families who have lived for generations on Mount Desert Island, the gateway to Acadia National Park. "Places that were going for $10,000 ten years ago are going for $80,000 to $90,000 today," says George Lawson, a retired fisherman. "There's no way that young people can stay in the town." The Maine State Housing Authority estimates that the number of Maine families able to afford an average home in the state fell from 81 percent in 1970 to 35 percent in 1990.

Residents of tourism-dependent resort communities are perhaps the hardest hit by rapid growth. In Vail, Colorado, three of every four dwellings are second homes occupied only a few months or weeks a year. Only 9 of Vail's 48 police and firefighters can afford to live in town.

The wave of migration to gateway communities also portends major changes for natural ecosystems and historically significant landscapes and towns. According to a recent report on resource problems facing the National Wildlife Refuge System, more than half the country's refuges, and the wildlife that depend on them, face threats to their health.

In Florida, widespread development of private lands bordering the National Key Deer Refuge has pushed the refuge's namesake, the endangered dwarf Key deer, to the brink of extinction. The Key deer is threatened not only by habitat loss but also by homeowners who feed the deer, drawing the animals to roadsides and residential areas, where every year vehicles kill as much as one-fifth of the Key deer population.

In Jackson Hole, Wyoming, residential subdivisions adjacent to the National Elk Refuge have diminished the wintering grounds of a herd of nearly 10,000 elk. "Sixty head of elk used to winter right where that house is," says refuge manager Mike Hedrick, pointing to a new housing tract on his border. The elk that winter on the refuge are the same animals that summer in

*Like many gateway communities, Jackson, Wyoming, is experiencing double-digit growth. Rapid development is displacing travel corridors and habitat for these elk, which have historically wintered in the National Elk Refuge. (Dennis Glick)*

the high country of nearby Yellowstone and Grand Teton National Parks, a prime attraction for the more than three million visitors a year.

A 1994 survey of national park superintendents revealed similar problems—85 percent of America's national parks are experiencing threats from outside their boundaries. Civil War battlefields are particularly vulnerable. A blue-ribbon congressional panel commissioned in 1991 to survey the condition of Civil War battle sites found that one-fifth of the nation's 400 most significant battlefields have been lost to development. Of the remaining battlefields, more than half are threatened. As the commission warned: "The nation's Civil War heritage . . . is disappearing under buildings, parking lots, and highways."

Even large parks are threatened. In 1994, a contagious strain of viral pneumonia killed more than two-thirds of a 100-animal herd of bighorn sheep that inhabits the eastern edge of Rocky Mountain National Park. According to the Colorado Division of Wildlife, development of private land adjacent to the park contributed to the spread of the disease by reducing

*In Petersburg, Virginia, this Civil War monument commemorating the siege of Petersburg is now surrounded by shopping malls and commercial development. More than 20 percent of the nation's 400 most significant Civil War battlefields have been lost to development. (Ed McMahon)*

available range and concentrating animals in remaining winter habitat. Stress caused by more frequent interactions with humans and pets also makes bighorns more susceptible to disease. "This park doesn't contain a complete ecosystem," says Rocky Mountain superintendent Homer Rouse. "We're inextricably linked with the lands on our borders."

## The Role of Gateway Communities

Gateway communities are important not simply because they provide places for Americans to eat or sleep during their visit to natural or historic areas. They also are portals to our most cherished landscapes. Here is where it is imperative that we integrate human needs with those of our natural environment or cultural history.

Gateway communities also offer important lessons for other rural communities grappling with growth and change. Ben Read, a writer in Jackson Hole, Wyoming, points out that these communities are perhaps the first to contend with absolute limits to growth in an area. While suburbs can simply shift growth to neighboring cities or counties, gateway communities don't have that option: Much of the land on their outskirts is publicly owned and thus off-limits to development. In an evermore crowded world, the lessons provided by gateway communities will be increasingly valuable to all.

Over the past few years, we talked with a variety of people in gateway communities across the country, listening to their experiences, concerns, and ideas. We also undertook an extensive survey of the land-use patterns and economic forces shaping gateway communities. Here's what we found:

1. Many gateway communities are overwhelmed by rapid growth that fails to meet local needs and aspirations.

2. The vast majority of residents in gateway communities, both longtime residents and newcomers, feel a strong attachment to the landscape and character of their town. They want a healthy local economy, but not at the expense of their natural surroundings or community character.

3. Many residents of gateway communities lack information about the land-use and economic-development options available to them. While reams of data and case studies have been produced for planners and landscape architects, there is an acute shortage of such information available to the laypeople making the day-to-day decisions about the future of their communities.

4. Perhaps most important, a number of gateway communities have already implemented successful initiatives that deal with growth in a manner that protects the community's identity while stimulating a healthy economy and safeguarding natural and historic areas. Throughout the country, dozens of communities have proved that economic prosperity doesn't have to rob them of character, degrade their natural surroundings, or transform them into tourist traps.

This book outlines the lessons and tools behind the many success stories we discovered. It is not a cry to stop all growth; nor is it a suggestion for gateway communities to accommodate any growth that presents itself. Rather, it's a call for each community to plan ahead so that growth meets local wishes, contributes to a sustainable economy, enhances a community's quality of life, and complements the neighboring park, wildlife refuge, or other public land.

As we move further into a new economic era characterized by global markets and instantaneous business communication, quality of life will become an increasingly important—maybe the most important—factor in attracting new employers and a skilled workforce. Today, businesses both large and small can operate virtually anywhere. Communities that take steps to protect their quality of life clearly enhance their economic potential as well.

In fact, if there is one theme underlying this book, it's that preserving what's special about America's communities and landscapes doesn't have to jeopardize local economic well-being. Study after study shows that communities that preserve their character and natural values consistently outperform the economies of those that don't.

For gateway communities, and indeed for every small town and city, the challenge is to retain a high quality of life in the face of often intense growth pressures—in short, to prevent a repeat of what happened in many of America's now undesirable and faceless suburbs. This book offers practical and proven lessons on how gateway communities can shape their futures. It describes economic development strategies, land-use planning processes, and conservation tools that gateway communities from all over the country have found effective. Each strategy or process is explained with examples from these communities. For readers who want more details, please consult the notes at the end of each chapter or refer to the suggestions for further reading at the back of the book.

Change is inevitable, but it does not have to come at the expense of what citizens and communities value. We can either be victims of change or we can plan for it, shape it, and emerge stronger from it. The choice is ours.

## Notes

**page 3:** For more information about the rising demand for second homes, see *American Recreational Property Survey*: 1995, by Ragatz Associates, sponsored by the International Timeshare Foundation; and "Redefining Resorts," by Ralph Bowden, *Urban Land*, August 1995, vol. 54, no. 8.

**page 3:** Figures on inheritances are from *Estimating the Size and Distribution of the Baby Boomers' Prospective Inheritances*, 1993, by Robert B. Avery and Michael S. Rendall, Department of Consumer Economics and Housing, Cornell University, Ithaca, New York.

**pages 3–4:** For information about rapid growth in Montana and the Rocky Mountains, see *Sustaining Greater Yellowstone: A Blueprint for the Future*, 1994, by Albert Harting, Dennis Glick, Chip Rawlins, and Bob Ekey, published by the Greater Yellowstone Coalition, P.O. Box 1874, Bozeman, Montana 59771, phone: (406) 586-1593. See also "Small Towns under Siege," *High Country News*, April 5, 1993, vol. 25, no. 6; and "The Rocky Mountain West at Risk," by Jeff Gersh, *Urban Land*, March 1995, vol. 54, no. 3.

**page 3:** The quote from George Lawson appears in *The Cumulative Impact of Development on Mount Desert Island, Maine*, 1988, by the Mount Desert Island League of Women Voters, P.O. Box 625, Southwest Harbor, Maine 04679, phone: (207) 244-5486.

**page 4:** See the following reports for information about the condition of our National Wildlife Refuge System: *National Wildlife Refuges: Continuing Problems with Incompatible Uses Call for Bold Action*, 1989, by the U.S. General Accounting Office (GAO/RCED- 89-196); *Fish and Wildlife Service Resource Problems: National Wildlife Refuges, National Fish Hatcheries, Research Centers*, 1983, by the U.S. Fish and Wildlife Service.

**pages 5–6:** For information about external threats to national parks, see *Activities Outside Park Borders Have Caused Damage to Resources and Will Likely Cause More*, 1994, by the U.S. General Accounting Office (GAO/RCED-94-59). Also, see *Report on the Nation's Civil War Battlefields*, 1993, prepared by the Civil War Sites Advisory Commission for the U.S. Senate Committee on Energy and Natural Resources, U.S. House of Representatives Committee on Natural Resources, and Secretary of the Interior.

Chapter 2

# The Economic Value of Quality of Life

*America's brightest people are attracted*
*by America's most beautiful places.*
—Colorado Governor Roy Romer

More and more gateway communities are finding that adjoining parks, wildlife refuges, or wilderness areas can be powerful economic assets. Tourism
is an obvious way to capitalize on nearby public lands. But parks, refuges,
and wilderness areas also are valuable for the contribution they make to
local quality of life.

*Quality of life* is a catchall term used to describe the noneconomic amenities a community has to offer, including clean air and water, safe streets,
open space, cultural events, recreational opportunities, uncongested roads,
good schools, and scenic views. Although the definition of quality of life may
vary from person to person, people of every ethnic and economic back-
ground place a high value on it. Surveys indicate that quality of life weighs
heavily in decisions people make about where they want to live and work.
Indeed, throughout the country Americans are fleeing blighted suburbs and
cities in search of cleaner, greener, smaller, safer, and more neighborly communities. Gateway communities are leading destinations.

Increasingly, Americans are saying that the place they live is as important
as what they do for a living—so much so that they're willing to relocate to a
"better" community even at the risk of diminished job opportunity or a lower
income. Technological advances like the fax machine, computer modem,
overnight delivery services, and electronic mail have accelerated this trend.

*Increasingly, Americans are saying that the place where they live is as important as what they do for a living. With their scenic beauty and high quality of life, gateway communities have become a magnet for millions of Americans looking to escape the congestion, banality, and faster tempo of life in the suburbs and cities. (Aspen Valley Land Trust)*

"People aren't just moving for jobs and money anymore," says Randy Shroll, an Idaho Department of Commerce official who recruits companies to relocate to the state. "They're moving because they want a decent place to live."

And companies are following them. A growing body of evidence suggests that quality of life is a dominant factor in attracting businesses. According to David Birch in his book *Job Creation in America: How the Smallest Companies Put the Most People to Work,* as much as 90 percent of the jobs in the American economy are being created by what he calls "high-innovation firms"—small firms that employ fewer than 20 employees. Birch maintains that these firms, which rely primarily on a skilled, intelligent work force, will locate in environments that "bright, creative people find attractive."

Even isolated communities with relatively high costs of living can attract these firms, as long as their quality of life is good enough to lure an educated workforce. "People used to move to find the jobs," says Randy Shroll, "but nowadays companies are moving to find the people."

Even larger corporations are following the lead of Birch's high-innovation firms. Springfield, Oregon, a community in the beautiful Willamette River Valley, recently attracted a new Sony Corporation compact disc factory that will provide 1,500 well-paying jobs. "It wasn't blind, dumb luck that helped us land Sony," says Mayor Bill Morrisette. "What we have here is quality of life. And as long as we don't screw that up, we'll always be able to attract people and businesses."

Similarly, in Jackson, Wyoming, gateway to Grand Teton and Yellowstone National Parks, the business with the largest payroll isn't a hotel or ski resort. It's the law firm of Spence, Moriarity and Schuster that has a national practice that allows it to be situated anywhere in the country. That the firm remains in Jackson—with a small airport and few local clients—is testimony to the quality of life the town offers.

Businesses in the country's highest growth industries—health care, computer software, electronics manufacturing, and professional services—are especially attracted to communities with a high quality of life. These firms rely heavily on employee satisfaction in guiding decisions about where to locate.

Nancy McMorrow's family moved its plastic manufacturing business from Long Island, New York—where the firm had been since 1956—to Belgrade, Montana, a community on the northern edge of the Yellowstone Ecosystem. "We fell in love with Montana," she says, "not just for the quality of life it offers, but for the skilled labor pool that's available and the can-do attitude of the people here." The firm brought 24 well-paying jobs to Belgrade.

For years, the conventional wisdom was that business owners weigh only economic factors when deciding where to locate a business: Will the business be able to obtain labor and capital? Will it have access to markets and transportation? Are raw materials nearby? What are the state and local tax rates?

But in a 1995 survey of business owners in communities adjacent to Yellowstone National Park, a team of economists found that businesses consider a great deal more when making decisions about where to locate. The traditional factors listed above, while cited by business owners as important, all ranked comparatively low in the decision-making process. In fact, even though two-thirds of the business owners surveyed felt they would be more profitable in an urban setting, 86 percent would choose to locate their business in the Yellowstone region again.

The reason? The area's high quality of life. According to business owners, the most important factors for locating or remaining in the Yellowstone region are, in order of importance: a quality environment, a good place to raise a family, and scenic beauty. "Firms locate in the Greater Yellowstone Ecosystem because of environmental, recreational, and community amenities, not for primarily business considerations," the study reported.

Business owners who were longtime residents of the region felt even stronger about this than newcomers, suggesting that a community's social, cultural, and environmental amenities are important not just for attracting new businesses, but also for retaining existing ones. The authors concluded that local policies that enhance and protect the amenities valued by residents and business owners will help communities to retain and attract businesses.

These findings apply in other rural areas as well: A community is more likely to enjoy a robust local economy if it adopts policies or initiatives that preserve its scenic, ecological, or historic assets. A 1992 study by the Massachusetts Institute of Technology found that by nearly every economic indicator, states with strong environmental policies consistently outperformed those with weak policies. For each state, MIT measured gross state product, total employment, construction employment, and labor productivity. Across the board, researchers found that policies promoting environmental quality do not hinder economic growth and development. In fact, they often advance it. "Highly skilled and well-educated workers tend to be attracted to regions that offer a better quality of life," the study concluded. "Thus, new industries, high-technology firms, and R&D laboratories may well migrate to environmentally strong states."

Another study, conducted by Bank of America in 1993, discovered that states with strong environmental policies have enjoyed more economic growth than those with weak ones. The company ranked each state according to its environmental standards. Over the last 15 years, states with strong environmental standards experienced an average economic growth rate of 2.60 percent per year, states with moderate standards 2.29 percent, and states with weak standards 2.15 percent. While these differences may seem small, they can be sizable over the long run. Bank of America concluded that public policies that protect a community's environment and quality of life help to sustain long-term economic growth.

A third study, this one done in 1994 by the Institute for Southern Studies in Durham, North Carolina, concluded that "The states that do the most to protect their natural resources also wind up with the strongest economies and the best jobs." Nearly all the states that ranked among the top dozen in environmental well-being also ranked highest in economic criteria. By the same token, states judged weakest on environmental standards were the worst economic performers.

Seizing upon the linkage between quality of life and economic growth, many gateway communities are adopting economic development strategies that build on their natural and cultural resources. Across the country, rural communities are casting a more critical eye at the old formulas for economic development, many of which have the potential to detract from the assets that contribute most to their economies.

In Dubois, Wyoming, for example, the local chamber of commerce opposed a U.S. Forest Service decision to allow oil and gas leasing on the neighboring Shoshone National Forest. The reason: Petroleum development could hinder Dubois's ability to attract and retain businesses dependent on the area's scenic beauty and environmental amenities. Just a few years ago, such an action would have been unthinkable. Surprised by the level of local opposition, the Forest Service scaled back the lease sales. "The Dubois economy depends on protecting wild lands and wildlife, our two most powerful and valuable resources," says Pat Neary, director of Fremont County's economic development programs.

Likewise, Madison County, Virginia, recently upheld scenic byway status for a two-lane highway that winds through 50 miles of farms and villages on the eastern flank of Shenandoah National Park and the Blue Ridge Mountains. County officials had considered rescinding the byway designation for Route 231 after several business owners complained it prohibited them from erecting "off-premise" signs. But an overwhelming number of businesses, including the county chamber of commerce and 46 merchants from Madison, the county seat, presented county supervisors with a petition urging Route 231's continued status as a scenic byway. An owner of a bed and breakfast testified to a three-fold increase in business since the byway's designation. The Virginia Department of Transportation estimates that scenic byway designation generates at least a 5 percent increase in tourist traffic.

Sitka, Alaska, is the gateway to Sitka National Historical Park, the site of an 1804 battle that cemented Russia's hold on Alaska. In 1993, Sitka's largest employer, a pulp mill, closed down. In a city of 8,500 people, more than 400 workers lost their jobs. "A lot of people predicted an economic downturn for us, but it never happened," says Larry Edwards, a former mill worker who now owns a local sea kayak shop. In fact, the closure of the mill may have actually helped Sitka by improving local air and water quality and forcing the community to diversify its economy. Having been burned once, Sitka is no longer willing to hitch its economy to a single industry. Besides embracing new tourism-oriented businesses like Edwards's kayak shop, the community also intends to retain its existing commercial fishing fleet, seafood processing plants, hospitals and health care firms, and value-added businesses that don't simply export raw commodities to other countries. "Sitka's economy is increasingly relying on the quality of the forest and environment," says Edwards.

## The Changing Global Economy
*by Ray Rasker, Ph.D., Economist*

To understand the economic forces reverberating through America's communities, it's first necessary to understand the momentous changes now taking place in the global economy. According to writer and analyst Peter Drucker, most economists agree that there are three trends currently shaping the world economy:

1. Manufacturers are using fewer raw materials in their products. Many of the most valuable products in the modern economy, including computer hardware, health care technology, and software, consume relatively few raw materials. Only 3 percent of the cost of producing a semiconductor chip, for example, is raw materials.

2. Thanks to a more productive workforce and more efficient manufacturing processes, there is less demand for physical labor. Instead, human resources are more often being dedicated to "knowledge-based" applications. For example, more than 80 percent of the expense of producing a modern automobile lies in its design, engineering, financing, patenting, and marketing.

3. Investment markets have become global. With the touch of a keyboard, billions of dollars can flow from one country to another. As a result, investment capital has no nationality; in today's economy, money follows good ideas regardless of where they occur on the globe.

These three forces are causing an upheaval in the way we do business. Trade is increasingly international, and it consists more of human resources, ideas, and financial capital than of raw materials.

One result of freer interchange of goods and services is that fewer and fewer products are made within a single country. Former Secretary of Labor Robert Reich liked to point out that a U.S. citizen looking for a new car and wanting to buy American would have a hard time doing so. For example, of the $10,000 purchase price of a Pontiac Le Mans, here's where the dollars go:

- $3,000 to South Korea for labor and assembly

- $1,750 to Japan for advanced components like engines, transaxles, and electronics

- $750 to Germany for styling and design

- $400 to Taiwan and Singapore for small components

- $250 to Britain for advertising and marketing services

- $50 to Ireland and Barbados for data processing

That leaves about $4,000, which is divided among executives in Detroit, lawyers and bankers in New York City, lobbyists in Washington, D.C., insurance and health care workers across the country, and General Motors shareholders all over the world. As Reich emphasizes, there is hardly a product made today that is not the result of a large, scattered, international assembly line.

So what does this mean for national economies? Plenty. In the past, a country's natural resource base and availability of labor and capital determined its comparative advantage in the world economy. Today, however, these production factors pale in comparison to a country's brainpower. What's important is not where the final product rolls off the assembly line, but who adds the most value to production. Japan, for example, is the wealthiest country in the world, even though it possesses relatively few natural resources.

In his book *Head to Head*, Lester Thurow predicts that the high-growth industries of the next few decades will be brainpower industries: microelectronics, biotechnology, telecommunications, machine tools, and computers and computer software. An important aspect of these industries is that they're "footloose"—they can locate anywhere in the world. Where they go is largely dependent on where their executives want to live and where they can attract a quality workforce.

Enter gateway communities. With their high quality of life, gateway communities are well positioned to attract the brainpower businesses predicted to be the growth industries of the future. To do so, however, gateway communities must retain the assets that give them an advantage over other communities.

## How Can Gateway Communities Enhance Quality of Life?

The lesson from this chapter is that gateway communities seeking to develop a vital local economy must ensure that growth and economic development don't come at the expense of their unique identity, quality of life, economic diversity, and fiscal well being. Communities that want to benefit from the world's changing economic realities need to make sure their quality of life remains high.

The good news is that any community can find ways to safeguard what its residents value. As demonstrated in the next chapter, there is a wide range of policy choices that can help a community preserve its natural areas and open space, support locally owned businesses, encourage traditional vocations, retain vibrant downtowns with a sense of character and tradition, and provide ample opportunity for outdoor recreation and other leisure activities.

The challenge is to retain a high quality of life in the face of mounting pressures for growth, homogeneity, and change. Without well-designed and publicly supported strategies to preserve their character and surroundings, gateway communities risk undermining the very assets responsible for their economic vitality and future potential. The recommendations found in chapters 3 and 4 offer some hints on how to ensure that growth doesn't jeopardize what residents of gateway communities cherish.

Case Study
======

## The Economy of the Greater Yellowstone Region

*Over the last two decades, the economy of the Greater Yellowstone region in Idaho, Montana, and Wyoming has shifted from extractive industries to services and government. What's happening in Yellowstone is occurring all over the country: Rural communities are relying increasingly on the natural lands surrounding them for the amenities they offer to residents rather than the raw materials they provide to commodity industries.*

The greater Yellowstone region of the northern Rocky Mountains spans three states—Idaho, Montana, and Wyoming—and some 18 million acres. More than 220,000 people live within its boundaries. The region also boasts some of the nation's most famous public lands: Yellowstone and Grand Teton National Parks, the National Elk and Hebgen Lake national wildlife refuges, and millions of acres of national forest wilderness areas, including the Wind River and Absaroka ranges.

The economic trends now shaping the communities in the greater Yellowstone region mirror those facing many other scenic areas of the United States. The region's amenities—its scenery, outdoor opportunities, and high quality of life—are promoting a new wave of economic and population growth. In fact, if the 20 counties within the Yellowstone region were considered as a separate state, they would be one of the nation's fastest growing.

The region's current growth cycle, however, differs from previous booms. Historically, the greater Yellowstone economy has been driven by commodity industries: mining, ranching, farming, and logging paid the bills. In 1969, these economic sectors accounted for one of every three workers in the region.

Over the last two decades, however, the economy of the Yellowstone region has undergone a metamorphosis. Although the region has added more than 66,000 new jobs since the mid-1970s, almost all the new job growth has been outside the commodity sectors of the economy. During the 1970s and 1980s, 96 percent of the region's new jobs—and 89 percent of its labor income—were in industries other than mining, logging, farming, ranching, or oil and gas development.

In fact, a 1997 high school or college graduate looking for work in the greater Yellowstone region would be most likely to find a job with a retail store, real estate office, bank or insurance firm, management consultant, school or college, engineering firm, health care provider, law firm, or in a branch of government. Today, the commodity industries employ just one of every six workers, half the level of 1969.

*In just a few decades, the economy of the greater Yellowstone region, including communities like Livingston, Montana, has shifted from extractive industries to the service and retail trade sectors. The same trends are facing gateway communities all over the country. (Dennis Glick)*

As local economies in the region have become less dependent on commodity industries, many residents have expressed concerns that employment opportunities will be limited to low-paying, menial jobs. All the evidence, however, suggests that these fears are unfounded.

Approximately 80 percent of the Yellowstone region's job gains since the mid-1970s came in the rapidly growing service sector of the economy, which admittedly does include relatively low-paying jobs like maids, busboys, and cashiers. In the greater Yellowstone region, however, the largest components of the service sector are in high-wage industries that offer an average salary of $21,547, nearly 20 percent more than the regional average of $18,030. The engineering and management component of the service sector, for example, makes up 29 percent of the new job growth in the region and provides an average salary of $39,376 per year. Likewise, the health care component comprises 22 percent of new job growth and provides an average salary of $20,443 per year.

The story isn't complete without a look at two more trends shaping the region's economy. First, increasing numbers of people are moving to scenic areas to retire. In the Yellowstone region, more than 35 percent of total personal income is now in the form of nonlabor earnings, primarily retirement income and money earned from past investments. That's up from 23 percent in 1970 and more than 2.5 times the total income derived from mining, logging, and agriculture. Second, big corporations are providing fewer jobs. Some 93 percent of the new businesses that commenced operations in the Yellowstone region between 1980 and 1990 were small firms with fewer than 20 employees.

What's happening in the Yellowstone economy is occurring all over the country: Rural communities are relying increasingly on the natural lands surrounding them for the amenities they offer to residents rather than the raw materials they provide to commodity industries.

Case Study
====
## Boulder, Colorado

*The secret to attracting high-paying businesses and industries often has less to do with a community's traditional economic factors than with its quality of life. Boulder, Colorado, boasts a first-class economy that rivals those of much larger cities. Many economists attribute Boulder's success in large part to its ambitious programs to protect public open space and create trails and parks for residents. Employers locate in Boulder because the city's many amenities make it easy to attract a top-notch workforce.*

Drive north out of Denver on Route 36 and in 30 minutes you'll arrive in Boulder, Colorado. Boulder's most prominent feature is the Flatirons, which tower over the city and form the first wall of the Rocky Mountain Front Range. Aptly named, these huge rock wedges seem like massive irons perched atop an ironing board, as if the gods had decided to rest in Boulder after pressing America's heartland into the Great Plains.

Home to the University of Colorado, Boulder is predominantly a college town—students comprise more than a quarter of the city's 90,000 people. Boulder is also an outdoors-oriented town: The city probably contains a higher percentage of mountain bikers, backpackers, runners, rock climbers, and skiers than any other community. Each of the city's residents seems to own a four-wheel-drive vehicle with a ski rack on the roof and a golden retriever in the back.

Boulder boasts a vibrant downtown with a strong business and retail sector. In 1977, the city converted a downtown thoroughfare into a pedestrian mall that on summer nights is crowded with thousands of residents and tourists who frequent its many shops, restaurants, and taverns. The city is also a hub for high-tech and service industries.

Boulder's scenic setting, its abundant recreational opportunities, and its proximity to mountain wilderness have attracted newcomers for decades. The first big wave of growth hit Boulder in the 1960s, when the city's population rose an astounding 80 percent. Rapid growth continued in the 1970s, with a 44 percent population increase. Although it exceeded 12 percent in the 1980s, growth has since tapered off.

Boulder was the first city in the West to enact land-use policies to protect its mountain setting from haphazard development. Nearly a century ago, in 1898, the city and county began purchasing land in the Flatirons. In 1958, a group of Boulder citizens convinced the city to discourage development in the mountains by curtailing water service to higher elevations. But the city's most significant conservation venture took place in 1967, when Boulder voters approved a 0.4 percent city sales tax—four-tenths of a cent on every dollar—to finance open-space acquisition. Three years earlier, Boulder's city council had quickly approved the purchase of a 155-acre mountainside property after the owner announced plans to build a resort overlooking the city. Residents didn't want to risk being caught off-guard again.

*Boulder, Colorado, uses a 0.7 percent sales tax to acquire open space and trail corridors, including this popular trail leading to the Flatirons. The city has acquired more than 25,000 acres of land through the tax. (Robert Glenn Ketchum)*

"Citizens here decided to preserve the city's mountain backdrop and protect what's special about Boulder," says Jim Crain, director of the city's open-space program. Using revenue from the sales tax, the city has purchased more than 25,000 acres of open space, riparian corridors, wildlife habitat, and conservation easements on farms and ranch land. All told, it has spent more than $90 million.

In 1989, voters reaffirmed their support for Boulder's open-space program by raising the sales tax to 0.73 percent. The margin of approval for the referendum was almost four to one. Today, more than $13 million a year is generated for the purchase of open space. "The impetus for the program came from the community," Crain points out. "You can't have a program like this imposed from the top."

Boulder couples its open-space acquisition program with a cap on the number of new residential building permits that can be issued each year and a restriction on its population growth to no more than 2 percent per year. In 1995, Boulder took steps to limit commercial development as well. From now on, the amount of nonresidential square footage built in the city will decrease by 5 percent each year.

U S West decided to locate its new Advanced Technologies Center in Boulder in part because of the city's natural and cultural amenities. Boulder proves that quality of life can be a dominant factor in attracting businesses. (U S West)

Boulder's success at managing growth has created a new set of challenges. Housing is relatively expensive due to the annual limits on residential building permits. And by slowing growth within its boundaries, the city has accelerated residential development in surrounding communities. As many as 40,000 people a day now commute into Boulder from growing towns like Broomfield, Lafayette, and Longmont.

All in all, however, Boulder demonstrates that local action and initiatives can help a community preserve what it values—in this case, mountain scenery, open space, and recreational opportunities—yet maintain an enviable economy. In fact, the city's current economic vitality is a direct result of its ambitious land-use planning, recreation, and conservation programs.

"Businesses have located in Boulder because it's a well-planned community with a lot of open space and recreational opportunities," says Crain. U S West is a case in point. In 1990, the telecommunications giant located a new research and development facility in Boulder, bringing 900 well-paying jobs to the city. "When U S West was looking for a new location, other communities offered them every incentive under the sun," says Crain. "In the end, they said it was Boulder's amenities that drew them here."

## Notes

page 10: Information about sources of new jobs is in *Job Creation in America: How the Smallest Companies Put the Most People to Work*, 1987, by David Birch, Free Press, New York.

page 11: Springfield, Oregon, Mayor Bill Morisette is quoted in "Oregon Thrives As It Protects Owls," 1994, by Timothy Egan, *The New York Times*, October 11, 1994, p. A1.

page 11: The study of business owners who locate in the Yellowstone area is titled "Travel-Stimulated Entrepreneurial Migration," 1995, by D. Snepenger, D. J. Johnson, and R. Rasker, *Journal of Travel Research*, vol. 34, no. 1, pp. 40–44.

page 12: The three studies linking environmental quality with economic well-being are *Environmentalism and Economic Prosperity: Testing the Environmental Impact Hypothesis*, 1992, by Dr. Stephen M. Meyer, Massachusetts Institute of Technology, Cambridge, Massachusetts; "Economic Growth and the Environment," by the Bank of America, published in *Economic and Business Outlook*, June/July 1993; and *The Gold and Green Report*, 1994, by Bob Hall, published by the Institute for Southern Studies, Durham, North Carolina. See also *Lost Landscapes and Failed Economies: The Search for a Value of Place*, 1996, by Thomas Michael Power, Island Press, Washington, D.C.

**page 14:** The citations from Dr. Ray Rasker's sidebar are *Post-Capitalist Society*, 1993, by Peter F. Drucker, HarperBusiness. New York, N.Y.; *The Work of Nations: Preparing Ourselves for 21st Century Capitalism*, 1991, by Robert B. Reich, Alfred A. Knopf, New York; *Head to Head: The Coming Economic Battle among Japan, Europe, and America*, 1993, by Lester Thurow, Morrow, New York.

**pages 16–18:** For more information on the Yellowstone-area economy, see *Regional Economic Information System*, 1994, by the U.S. Department of Commerce, Bureau of the Census, Washington, D.C.; *County Business Patterns: Idaho, Montana, Wyoming*, 1994, by the U.S. Department of Commerce, Bureau of Economic Analysis, Washington, D.C.; *County Economic Profiles of the Greater Yellowstone Region*, 1993, compiled by Stewart Mitchell from information collected by the U.S. Department of Commerce, published by the Greater Yellowstone Coalition and The Wilderness Society.

**pages 18–20:** For more information on Boulder's open-space program, contact the City of Boulder Open Space Department, P.O. Box 791, Boulder, Colorado 80306, phone: (303) 441-3440.

# Chapter 3

## Tourism: Bane or Boon?

Tourism is a leading employer in most gateway communities. It's likely to remain so for some time, given that visitation to parks, historic sites, wildlife refuges, and other public lands has been rising steadily since the end of World War II. In 1970, about 172 million people visited the national parks; by 1995, that number had soared to 270 million. Similar trends can be seen in visitation to national forests. The Forest Service recently changed the way it records visits, so information compiled before 1990 can't be compared to current records. The numbers from the early 1990s, however, show astonishing growth. In 1994, the national forests registered 835 million visits, up from 598 million in 1991—an increase of nearly 40 percent. (Although the number of people visiting national wildlife refuges remains at a steady 25–30 million a year, the U.S. Fish and Wildlife Service has recently begun to promote a wider variety of recreational activities at refuges, which, according to Nancy Marx of the agency's Division of Refuges, is expected to lead to an increase in visitation.)

Officials at public land agencies attribute the surge in visitation to several factors, including increasing numbers of retired Americans with more leisure time, growing amounts of international visitors, and better access to, and information about, public lands. With visitation showing no sign of abating, gateway communities can expect tourism to remain a vital component of their local economy. But every gateway community also should take steps to ensure that tourism remains just *one* element of the local economy, not the *only* element.

Economists disagree about nearly everything, but they do agree that the more diverse an economy is, the more likely it will be able to withstand downturns. An economy overly dependent on one source of income—be it tourism, agriculture, or coal mining—is more susceptible to boom-and-bust cycles, changes in consumer preferences, and other market forces. That said, rule number one for any community looking to expand tourism's contribution to the local economy should be to make sure that tourism won't displace existing industries and businesses. Before looking for new economic opportunities, a community needs to keep the jobs it has. Tourism should never be viewed as an industry that can replace the economic benefits of a sawmill, a commercial fishing fleet, a small manufacturing firm, or a vital agricultural community. All too often, however, local officials actively promote tourism at the expense of other economic sectors, despite growing evidence that tourism is not the panacea it appears to be.

Tourism has three shortfalls:

1. It's a highly seasonal and low-paying industry. Unlike other industries, tourism rarely provides the wage levels needed to support a family. In addi-

*Without care, tourism—and the crowds it can generate—can overwhelm a community and displace other economic sectors. Gateway communities need to make sure that tourism is just one element, not the only element, of the local economy. (Robert Glenn Ketchum)*

tion, it suffers from downtimes when local businesses and merchants will find it hard to keep their doors open.

Once a sleepy little town in the Ozark Mountains, Branson, Missouri, is now the nation's most popular destination for bus coach tours and the second-most popular destination for automobile travelers. The draw is entertainment—the city has 36 country music theaters that host stars like Kenny Rogers, the Osmonds, and Mel Tillis. While tourism provides employment for three-quarters of the city's 5,000 residents, the jobs are primarily low paying and seasonal—unemployment surges to 20 percent in the five-month off-season. Moreover, affordable housing is becoming a problem. Although Branson has so far kept property taxes from escalating, in some parts of the city the cost of land now exceeds $300,000 an acre. The upshot: Despite the city's newfound economic prosperity, 71 percent of residents think Branson used to be a better place to live, according to a 1995 survey reported in *The Economist*.

2. Large-scale tourism requires considerable investment in services and infrastructure, such as parking lots, law enforcement officers, medical facilities, and sewage treatment plants. During peak tourist seasons, a rural community of a few thousand people can find itself in need of services and infrastructure capable of handling crowds far in excess of its year-round population. Paying for these, of course, requires the local government to increase property or sales taxes.

In the 1980s, Moab, Utah, began a nationwide campaign to attract tourists interested in mountain biking, river rafting, and backpacking on the public lands that surround it. The effort was a success—too much so. Moab's population of 5,000 now soars to 16,000 during the spring and summer tourist season. The city's law enforcement costs are four times higher than what they were in 1978, even though the resident population is the same. What's more, the county government now has to build a new state-of-the art landfill because waste levels are too high to allow continued use of its dump. "Instead of using our existing site," says County Commissioner Bill Hedden, "we have to construct a Class I landfill at a cost in excess of a million dollars." Moab's popularity has also fueled a boom in the local real estate market: Houses are selling for five and six times what they cost in the 1980s, and property taxes have tripled, making it difficult for long-time residents to afford to live in town. Local leaders now question whether tourism is the economic savior it once appeared to be.

3. A tourism-based economy supercharged by heavy promotion often creates a community in which longtime residents can no longer afford to live. Sometimes, they may not care to live there even if they could.

Former mining town Telluride, Colorado, is now a pricey resort for movie stars and other wealthy out-of-towners. Nearly 70 percent of the town's 500 housing units are second homes vacant most of the year. Spurring the change was a jet-service airport that opened in 1985 and made Telluride easily accessible to people all over the world. Most of the town's residents from the 1960s and 1970s have left, some because they could no longer afford a house in the community (where the average price of a home is $300,000, second in Colorado only to Aspen), others because they didn't care to remain in glitzy Telluride.

In some communities, residents have said enough is enough. In 1994, citizens in Jackson Hole, Wyoming, voted to discontinue a bed and lodging tax that the local chamber of commerce used to promote tourism in the region. The 2 percent tax, which had been in place since 1986, generated $1.3 million a year for advertising Jackson Hole as a vacation destination. "People here would be more than delighted to have a lodging tax, but they want it used for improvements in the community dealing with the impacts of tourism and growth," says Bill Phelps, who runs a mail-order hunting-equipment store in Jackson and who spearheaded the campaign to eliminate the tax. "We don't want the tax used to attract more people. The sewer plant we built just 10 years ago is already at capacity because it can't handle our population in August."

## Weighing Tourism as an Option

There are many ways for gateway communities to benefit from tourism without transforming themselves into tourist traps, entertainment centers, or resort communities for out-of-towners. Gateway communities weighing tourism as an economic development option should consider the following four criteria:

1. *Economic Diversity*: Is tourism part of a larger strategy of diverse economic development, or is it being viewed as a panacea, the latest answer to the community's economic woes? At what level can tourism be encouraged before it begins to drive out other economic engines?

2. *Fiscal Cost*: Can the community embrace tourism without assuming a large fiscal burden, such as new investments in law enforcement officers, parking lots, medical facilities, or a multimillion-dollar waste-disposal system?

3. *Sustainability*: Is tourism compatible with protecting the community's natural resources, or will it degrade scenery and water quality, disrupt fish and wildlife, and lead to increased trash and litter? By the same token, can tourism take place without destroying the character of the community, or will it inflate property values and transform the community into a resort in which residents can no longer afford to live?

4. *Quality*: Will tourism provide meaningful employment for local people? Does it offer visitors an authentic look at the community's distinctive assets and history, or is it "tourist trap" development that provides low-paying jobs for residents and glitz and amusement for visitors?

Examples of tourist attractions that meet these criteria include scenic highways, wildlife preserves, historic sites, and outdoor adventure locations.

## Scenic Highways

Roads and highways that traverse scenic countryside can be a huge economic boost to the communities they link. The U.S. Travel Data Center estimates that every mile of a designated "scenic highway" generates between $30,000 and $35,000 in tourist spending annually. Every year, more than 20 million people travel on the 469-mile-long Blue Ridge Parkway—which connects Shenandoah National Park with Great Smoky Mountains National Park in North Carolina. These motorists pump more than $1.3 billion a year

*Winding between Shenandoah National Park in Virginia and Great Smoky Mountains National Park in Tennessee, the Blue Ridge Parkway pumps more than $1.3 billion a year into the counties it adjoins. The Virginia Department of Transportation estimates that a scenic highway designation produces at least a 5 percent increase in tourist traffic. (Ed McMahon)*

into the counties adjoining the parkway, generating nearly $98 million in tax revenue for local governments and supporting more than 26,500 jobs.

Communities wishing to explore scenic highway designation should look for exceptional road segments in their area. The most popular scenic highways are those where several communities have teamed up to create a travel experience lasting for more than just a day. A brochure about the highway can be used both as a guide to the traveler and as an advertising tool for local businesses. Federal highway dollars from the Intermodal Surface Transportation Efficiency Act, better known as ISTEA, are available for help with design and signage.

## Wildlife Preserves

Polls of visitors to national parks and wildlife refuges indicate that most people hope to catch a glimpse of wildlife. According to the U.S. Department of Commerce, wildlife-related tourism generates nearly $60 billion a year for the U.S. economy. Across the country, many communities have already set aside wildlife-viewing areas, preserved or acquired access to hunting and fishing areas, or created wildlife museums to help visitors understand local ecology.

*Two photographers track a moose. Wildlife-related tourism, including hunting, fishing, and wildlife watching, generates nearly $60 billion a year for the U.S. economy. (John Turner)*

Consider Tyrrell County, North Carolina, which lies at the center of a half-million-acre network of public lands that includes six national wildlife refuges. Like many gateway communities, Tyrrell County found that its proximity to public lands could help jump start the local economy. Neighboring wildlife refuges are now the centerpiece of an ambitious economic development plan that aims to make Columbia, the county seat, a gateway for visitors interested in wildlife-watching, hunting, fishing, and outdoor recreation.

Bird-watching is an often overlooked source of tourism income. Bird-watchers in search of species they've never seen before won't hesitate to travel long distances and spend lots of money. A 1995 study of communities bordering national wildlife refuges found that birders generated between half-a-million and several million dollars a year of economic benefits in each community. The table below illustrates the economic impact that birders had in 1994 at these communities.

Recognizing the economic potential of bird-watching, nearly 50 North American communities—many of them gateway communities—host annual events to attract birders. In 1994, Harlingen, Texas, a gateway to the Laguna Atascosa National Wildlife Refuge and a stopping point for migrating water birds, began an annual birding gala that in 1995 drew 1,800 people and pumped $1.6 million into the local economy. Every November, Socorro, New Mexico, the gateway to the Bosque del Apache National Wildlife Refuge and a rest stop for thousands of sandhill cranes and snow geese, sponsors a Festival of the Cranes, which in 1994 attracted more than 14,000 people. Concrete, Washington, a gateway to Mt. Baker National

**The Economic Impact of Bird-Watchers in Nine Gateway Communities (1994)**

| Community | Refuge | Visiting birders | Local economic impact ($) |
|---|---|---|---|
| McAllen, Tex. | Santa Ana | 99,000 | 14.4 million |
| Chincoteague, Va. | Chincoteague | 95,970 | 9.7 million |
| Oak Harbor, Ohio | Ottawa | 193,500 | 5.6 million |
| Burns, Ore. | Malheur | 50,000 | 4.0 million |
| Rio Hondo, Tex. | Laguna Atascosa | 48,000 | 4.0 million |
| Oceanville, N.J. | Edwin B. Forsythe | 98,038 | 4.0 million |
| Socorro, N.Mex. | Bosque del Apache | 90,788 | 3.3 million |
| Calipatria, Calif. | Salton Sea | 54,000 | 3.1 million |
| Hartford, Kan. | Quivara | 17,400 | 636,000 |

*Source:* U.S. Fish and Wildlife Service

Forest, celebrates the annual return of bald eagles to the Skagit River Valley, site of one of the largest concentrations of eagles in the lower 48, with a three-day festival that attracts 2,000 people.

Mio, Michigan, proves that bird-watchers aren't just interested in high-profile species like eagles and cranes. Since 1993, Mio has hosted an annual Kirtland's Warbler Festival that draws 7,000 people to view an endangered songbird that breeds exclusively in the jack pines of central Michigan's Huron National Forest.

## The Economic Impact of Wildlife Habitat

Today there are more than 500 national wildlife refuges in all 50 states. Hunting is allowed in almost two-thirds of them, and most offer abundant opportunities for fishing, wildlife-viewing, and other recreational pursuits.

• According to the U.S. Fish and Wildlife Service, which manages the refuge system, 108 million people take part in wildlife-related recreation each year. In 1991, annual expenditures by these people totaled nearly $60 billion, with more than two-thirds of that spent on hunting and fishing.

• Americans spend $18 billion a year to watch wildlife, triple what they spend on movies or sporting events. Bird-watchers alone spend $5.2 billion a year, according to studies by the U.S. Fish and Wildlife Service.

• According to the 1994 Roper Survey on Outdoor Recreation, fishing is the favorite recreational activity of American men. In 1991, anglers spent $24 billion or an average of $674 each. Every year more than 30 million Americans purchase fishing licenses.

### Historic Sites

Increasing numbers of families want to include an educational point of interest or history lesson as part of their vacation. According to surveys by the U.S. Travel Data Center, tourists cite cultural heritage as one of the top three factors in choosing their vacation destination. As a way of attracting these tourists, many communities have designated walking tours of historic downtowns, published maps and guides to historic sites in the area, or created exhibits on local history.

In Fredericksburg, Virginia, the site of four Civil War battles, the city council's efforts to preserve historic buildings and architecture have strengthened tourism's contribution to the local economy. In the early 1970s, Fredericksburg was mired in an economic slump, with few battlefield tourists venturing downtown, and businesses fleeing the city for outlying areas. To reverse this decline and control the demolition and renovation of buildings, the city in 1972 designated most of its downtown as a historic district. As incentives for businesses to relocate downtown, the city waived requirements that stores provide customer parking and initiated a small grants program to help property owners restore historic façades. The result: a bustling downtown with few vacancies and a tourism industry that contributes $42.9 million a year to the local economy, all in a way that enhances the city's unique character.

Industrial history is a new attraction. People often want to tour old mills, mines, or factories. Many communities have produced brochures and booklets that describe how a local industry furthered the development of their state or the nation. Lowell, Massachusetts, and Butte, Montana, are just two examples of gateway communities capitalizing on their industrial pasts. (See the next chapter for more details on what they have done.)

## The Economic Impact of Historic Preservation

Many communities have historical and cultural resources that, properly protected or restored, can significantly enhance their economy and quality of life. What follows is a sampler of facts and figures from *The Economics of Historic Preservation: A Community Leader's Guide*, by Donovan D. Rypkema (Preservation Press, 1995).

*Property Values.* A study by the Government Finance Officers Association found that property values in historic districts in Galveston, Texas, and Fredericksburg, Virginia, increased at a rate from 1.5 to 5 times higher than in comparable areas. Not a single study has shown that historic districts lead to a decline in property values.

*Income to the Community.* One million dollars invested in rehabilitation versus one million dollars in new construction means that

- $120,000 more will stay in the community
- $34,000 more in retail sales in the community
- $107,000 more in household incomes
- as many as nine more construction jobs will be created in the community and five more jobs elsewhere

*Life Expectancy.* The life expectancy of most contemporary buildings is 30 to 40 years, considerably less than the life expectancy of an older building that is restored or rehabilitated.

*Cost Savings.* It costs 4 percent less to rehabilitate an older building than to construct a new one. If demolition of an older building is required before construction of a new one, the savings can be as much as 16 percent.

### Outdoor Adventure Locations

Outdoor and adventure travel are the fastest growing segments of the U.S. travel industry. Travel agents once joked that outdoor types arrived in a pair of worn-out shorts with a $20 bill in the pocket—when they left a week later, neither had been changed. Nowadays, outdoor enthusiasts arrive with $1,000 mountain bikes, canoes, or skis strapped to the roofs of their brand new sport-utility vehicles. During the day they look for challenging bicycling, hiking, rafting, skiing, or rock climbing, but at night they want a good meal, entertainment, and top-notch accommodations.

Communities can attract adventure travelers by developing trails and bicycle routes, acquiring public boat launches and parking areas, or preserving the integrity of natural areas. New businesses like bicycle shops, canoe and kayak stores, hunting and fishing guides, ski shops, and climbing outfitters are likely to spring up in adventure travel hot spots.

Case Study
==========

## Townsend and Pittman Center, Tennessee

*Can a community enjoy the benefits of tourism without sacrificing its character to commercial forces? On the boundary of Great Smoky Mountains National Park, Tennessee, the towns of Townsend and Pittman Center have found that uniting residents behind a vision for the future enables them to reap the benefits of tourism without losing what they love about their towns. That contrasts sharply with nearby Pigeon Forge and Gatlinburg, where high-powered, high-volume tourism has transformed those two communities into amusement parks.*

Gatlinburg, Tennessee, has changed a great deal from the small community immortalized by Johnny Cash in the song "A Boy Named Sue." Cash sings of a vengeful young man scouring the Smoky Mountains for the no-good father that named him Sue:

> Well, it was Gatlinburg in mid-July,
> I'd just hit town and my throat was dry,
> I thought I'd stop and have myself a brew.
> At an old saloon on a street of mud,
> There at a table dealing stud,
> Sat the dirty, mangy dog that named me Sue.

In today's Gatlinburg, a stranger would be hard pressed to find the dirt roads and old saloons of which Cash sings. A busy four-lane highway divides the town, and the locally owned bars and restaurants have long since given way to fast-food franchises and chain motels. Even dirty, mangy dogs are few and far between.

As portals to Great Smoky Mountains National Park, Gatlinburg and nearby Pigeon Forge are perhaps the country's best examples of gateway communities completely transformed by tourism. Factory outlet stores hawk everything from cowboy boots to designer dresses, while amusement parks, wax museums, and t-shirt shops cater to people of all ages. Go-cart racing is the latest rage; at least 11 ovals are available. More adventurous types can visit a vertical wind tunnel that simulates indoor skydiving, play laser tag in a 9,000-square-foot arcade, or jump off a five-story bungee tower.

Country-music halls and theme parks also are popular. Enjoy that lonesome sound at Bonnie Lou and Buster's Hayride Country Show, Phil Campbell's Hee Haw Show, Dollywood, the Great American Opry, the Lonesome Dove Dance Hall, the Music Mansion Theater, the Rainbow Jamboree, or the Smoky Mountain Jamboree (not to be confused with the Smoky Mountain *Jubilee*. For rock-and-rollers, there's an Elvis museum.

Gatlinburg and Pigeon Forge exhibit a problem faced by many gateway communities: As the local economy grows increasingly dependent on mass-marketing, entertainment, and tourism, traditional industries and long-time residents are forced out by rising property values and the higher taxes that

*Transformed into a community completely dependent upon tourism, Pigeon Forge, Tennessee, generates an amazing amount of tax revenue, but its economy consists almost entirely of low-paying, seasonal jobs. (Robert Glenn Ketchum)*

accompany them. Even though both towns generate an amazing amount of tax revenue, their economies consist almost entirely of seasonal, low-paying service jobs, not the permanent positions needed to support a family.

A few major landowners have reaped big profits from phenomenal increases in property values, but those same increases have driven out many long time residents unable to afford housing in the area. In fact, Gatlinburg no longer has any residential neighborhoods—virtually all housing in the town has been converted to rental property or second homes.

Haphazard development of private land in the shadow of Great Smoky Mountains National Park also takes its toll on the region's magnificent scenery and natural resources. The roads into the Smoky Mountains are lined with bumper-to-bumper traffic and hundreds of billboards. In Gatlinburg, views of the Smokies have been marred by an observation tower, scores of high-rise condominium developments, an aerial tramway, and a 15-story hotel, which, while boasting of its "spectacular views," spoils the view for everyone else.

Worse are the impacts that development has on the park's wildlife—the original attraction for visitors. Every autumn, black bears migrate out of the park in their quest for food to build fat reserves for the long winter. But the rush to find building sites near the park has sealed off important migration corridors necessary for the bears to reach feeding grounds, according to Dr. Mike Pelton, a bear biologist at the University of Tennessee. "In the fall, a primary food source for the bears is oak acorns found at lower elevations outside the park," Pelton says. "In real crunch years of scarce food, bears migrating out of the park are getting killed on highways or shot in backyards."

Is every gateway community destined to become like Gatlinburg and Pigeon Forge? Clearly not.

Fifteen miles south of Gatlinburg is Townsend (pop. 350), another town bordering the park. Positioning itself as an alternative to the glitter of its neighbors, Townsend has adopted the slogan "The peaceful side of the Smokies." The town's appeal lies not in bungee jumping, go-cart racing, or factory outlets, but in its natural amenities: cool, clear rivers for fishing and floating; family-owned and -operated lodges; a colorful history; scenic trails and country roads for hiking, biking, and horseback riding; and a chance to see a black bear or white-tailed deer in the wild.

"Most of the people here don't want Townsend to become like Gatlinburg," says City Councilwoman Sandy Headrick. "We don't want to live in a town with traffic jams and Dollywoods and water slides."

Just north of Gatlinburg is the small town of Pittman Center (pop. 500), which also has successfully preserved its character. In 1989, Pittman Center residents convened a series of public meetings designed to produce a shared vision for their future. They decided to prohibit billboards and garish signs, limit commercial development to the town's core, and protect the flow and quality of the Little Pigeon River, which runs through town.

To realize this vision, Pittman Center enacted several widely supported ordinances. One limits development of hillsides and steep slopes. "We've tried to recognize that real estate which is hard to develop shouldn't be developed," says Jim Coykendall, an architect who has lived in Pittman Center since 1969.

Another ordinance places size limits on signs and prohibits billboards so that the community's streets and highways remain uncluttered. Leading by example, Pittman Center's street signs are made of wood rather than metal. And the first thing visitors see is an attractive wooden sign that reads "Pittman Center—A Community Dedicated to Preserving Our Mountain Heritage."

Coykendall attributes Pittman Center's success not only to the public's involvement in the visioning process, but also to the local people who have made sure the community follows up on its ideas. "If you can get just four or five people to commit the time and the effort, they can bring the rest of the community along," he says. "You can always get outside assistance, but the process has got to be driven from inside the community."

*Contrast Pigeon Forge with neighbor Pittman Center, which has managed to prosper while preserving its rural character and surroundings. This sign signals the community's desire to protect its heritage. (Luther Propst)*

Can places like Townsend and Pittman Center preserve their unique qualities and still enjoy a healthy economy? According to Townsend City Councilwoman Sandy Headrick, the answer is a resounding yes. "There's a lot of room for controlled growth," she says. "We think we can have a good business sector and still maintain the peace and quiet that we have here now."

Case Study
=======

# Gettysburg, Pennsylvania

*Tourism is the bread and butter for many communities that border national parks, wildlife refuges, and other public lands. Without care, though, tourism can destroy the very assets that attract visitors in the first place. In Gettysburg, city officials and residents have worked with Gettysburg National Military Park to protect and restore the integrity of the country's most visited battlefield. The Park Service has repaid the favor by helping the community restore the historical character of its downtown, thereby allowing Gettysburg businesses to capture more of the park's visitors.*

Gettysburg lies just over the Yankee side of the Mason–Dixon line at the crossroads of the North and South. It was here in 1863 that Union troops dashed General Robert E. Lee's hopes for a decisive victory in the North, repelling the Rebel army and returning the conflict to Confederate soil. More than any other battle, Gettysburg marked the turning point of the Civil War.

In 1895, Congress commemorated the battle by establishing the Gettysburg National Military Park, thereby preserving the hills and fields where the Blue and the Gray clashed. For more than a century, Americans have flocked here to witness the site of this monumental event in our history. In 1863, 15,000 people came to hear Lincoln deliver his legendary Gettysburg address. Today, the battlefield hosts more than 1.7 million visitors a year.

If Gettysburg is America's most acclaimed Civil War battlefield, it is also its most commercialized. As long ago as 1977, the National Advisory Council on Historic Preservation described the highway leading into Gettysburg as "a monument to the importance of the hamburger in American life." Today, a tour guide standing on Cemetery Ridge could point west and say, "Pickett's men charged through that line of motels, confronting Union troops at that fried-chicken stand. The first line faltered in the Burger King parking lot and regrouped next to the Tastee-Freez."

Gettysburg residents now realize that commercial exploitation of the area's historical assets threatens the very attributes that make it such a powerful attraction. Unwilling to accept a future as a tourist trap, the citizens of

Gettysburg have opted to restore the battlefield's integrity. First, local leaders suggested that the park identify the private lands most important to interpreting and understanding the battle. In 1990, Congress used the information to designate a "Gettysburg Historic District"—11,000 acres of privately owned buildings, homes, and farms surrounding the park.

While the new law prohibits the Park Service from acquiring land within the historic district, it does authorize park officials to accept donations of conservation easements on properties within it. Under the law, the Park Service also provides landowners and local governments with financial assistance and free advice about conservation tools, landscaping, and historic preservation. In 1995, the Park Service awarded more than $95,000 to local projects to design signs and educational materials, improve regional transportation systems, and update municipal historic preservation ordinances.

Congress also realized that to fully protect the battlefield, the park needed to acquire some 1,900 acres adjacent to its boundary, including a controversial 310-foot-tall observation tower on private land next to the park's visitor center. The tower, which was erected in 1972, can be seen from nearly everywhere on the battlefield. One of the park's current priorities is to purchase and raze the tower. Because of federal budget shortfalls, however, the Park Service must raise the funds from private sources.

Built by a private developer, this observation tower at Gettysburg National Military Park, Pennsylvania, dominates nearly every vantage point on the battlefield. Gettysburg's business community now realizes that protecting the integrity of the battlefield is in their best interest. (Ed McMahon)

Community members welcome the Park Service's cooperative attitude. "We've seen a big change here in the way the Park Service interacts with the community," says Peg Weaver, director of the Gettysburg–Adams County Area Chamber of Commerce. Community leaders are reciprocating. "For the first time ever," Weaver says, "we've nominated a Park Service official to serve on the Chamber of Commerce's board of directors."

Gettysburg's business sector hopes the ongoing efforts to safeguard local character will also induce more park visitors to stop in the town. In 1994, the park's economic impact on the local economy was nearly $111 million, including $100.4 million in visitor expenditures and $6.5 million in state and local tax revenues. Gettysburg wants to tap the park for an even greater economic boost, not by bringing in more tourists, but by convincing visitors to stay longer and to patronize downtown attractions and businesses.

Currently, only about half the 1.7 million annual visitors to the park continue on to historic sites in downtown Gettysburg. Because visitors come to relive history, the best way for the town to attract them is to ensure a visit to an authentic community. Accordingly, the town is working to restore historic buildings, enhance the streets and corridors that link the town and park, and emphasize the community's role in the battle by erecting statues and other interpretive displays.

At the request of local officials, the Park Service also provides comments on every development project proposed in the historic district. "They like to

One of the National Park Service's goals at Gettysburg is to help the city's businesses capture more of the park's visitors. This historic marker in downtown Gettysburg was paid for in part by a Park Service grant. (Paul Witt)

hide behind us as a way to improve proposals," says Joe DiBello, a Park Service planner in Philadelphia.

Citizens groups are helping, too. In 1995, a partnership composed of Friends of Gettysburg, the National Park Service, and three local utilities agreed to finance the burial of more than three miles of overhead power lines along the main road through the battlefield. The partnership raised more than $200,000 in private donations.

Underlying the success at Gettysburg is the park's contribution to the economic well-being of the entire community. "People here now recognize the many advantages of keeping the battlefield intact," says Peg Weaver, "Every dollar spent there eventually filters back to the community."

## The Economic Benefits of Protecting Battlefields

Many gateway communities are located adjacent to historic battlefields, which provide a number of important economic benefits:

- A battlefield can be a basic industry that provides jobs in a community.

- Battlefields can generate income from visitor purchases and sales tax revenue. In 1994, tourists at Gettysburg National Military Park, Pennsylvania, generated $100.4 million in visitor expenditures and $6.5 million in state and local tax revenues. Even a lesser known battlefield, like Pea Ridge in Arkansas, generates as much as $10.8 million a year.

- Every dollar spent in a community is spent again in the community at least twice. For example, at Pea Ridge, the $10.8 million in annual visitor expenditures had a total economic impact of $20.2 million.

- Expenditures by agencies that manage battlefields bring money into communities. Below are the National Park Service's 1993 operating budgets for several Civil War battlefields:

| Battlefield | Annual budget ($) |
| --- | --- |
| Gettysburg, Pennsylvania | 3.3 million |
| Fredericksburg and Spotsylvania, Virginia | 2.8 million |
| Petersburg, Virginia | 1.5 million |
| Chickamauga, Georgia | 1.5 million |
| Vicksburg, Mississippi | 1.5 million |
| Manassas, Virginia | 1.0 million |
| Richmond, Virginia | 950,000 |
| Wilson's Creek, Missouri | 830,000 |
| Kennesaw Mountain, Georgia | 792,000 |
| Shiloh, Tennessee | 760,000 |
| Pea Ridge, Arkansas | 469,000 |

Source: The Conservation Fund: *Dollars and $ense of Battlefield Preservation: The Economic Benefits of Protecting Civil War Battlefields* (1994).

## Case Study

# Tyrrell County, North Carolina

*Rural areas often lack the ability to attract high-paying industries. What many do have is an abundance of wild lands and recreational opportunities. In rural Tyrrell County, North Carolina (pop. 4,000), residents teamed up with the U.S. Fish and Wildlife Service and the state to help augment their economy with eco-tourism. The result has been a new source of jobs and income for local residents in a way that improves the county's environment and quality of life.*

Tyrrell County lies at the center of a half-million-acre network of natural areas that includes six national wildlife refuges: Alligator River, Cedar Island, Lake Mattamuskeet, Pocosin Lakes, Roanoke River, and Swanquarter. The refuges are critical not only for migratory birds but also for endangered wildlife like the red wolf, which was reintroduced here in 1993.

Although rich ecologically, Tyrrell County is one of the poorest counties in North Carolina. The unemployment rate hovers around 20 percent, and many of the county's 4,000 residents rely on low-paying seasonal work.

Decades of hard times convinced county residents that if they were going to improve the local economy, they'd have to start capitalizing on the resources they had at hand. "Sure, it would be nice to have a lot of large employers and jobs around here," says J. D. Brickhouse, the county administrator. "But without a larger and more skilled workforce, we're not going to get the IBMs or GEs. We've got to look at the situation realistically."

Like other gateway communities, Tyrrell County turned to its vast acres of unspoiled lands. The region's six national wildlife refuges are now the centerpiece of an ambitious eco-tourism plan that aims to make Columbia, the county seat, the starting point for visitors interested in outdoor recreation and wildlife experiences.

Every year, two million people drive through Columbia on their way to beaches on North Carolina's Outer Banks, just an hour to the east. With tourists already in the area, Tyrrell County simply had to figure out how to get them out of their cars.

The 1990 establishment of Pocosin Lakes National Wildlife Refuge provided the needed spark. After the federal government acquired the 114,000-acre refuge, a gift from the Richard King Mellon Foundation, Congress authorized construction of a new visitor center to help offset the impact of removing private land from the local tax base. When completed, the visitor center will be the starting point for tours of the region's natural areas. It will feature state-of-the-art exhibits on the region's natural and cultural history; a research station; and an environmental education facility, the Center for the Sounds, complete with auditoriums, classrooms, and a dormitory for students and teachers.

"A visitor center will be able to attract some of the people who now drive through the county without stopping," says Jim Savery, refuge manager at Pocosin Lakes.

Because it could take several years for Congress to allocate funds for the center, county leaders convinced the state to lend a hand in the meantime. In 1994, the North Carolina Department of Transportation completed construction of a highway rest area and visitor center in Columbia. There, a series of exhibits and displays helps tourists learn about the region's many attractions. To make it easier for people to visit downtown Columbia, Tyrrell County also built a new mile-long boardwalk that begins at the rest stop then winds its way along the Scuppernong River and through the downtown business district.

Travelers who want to see more of the river can enjoy the Scuppernong River greenway, a 27-mile web of canoe trails, bicycle routes, and walking paths created in 1994 with grants from the state and two private foundations. To publicize the greenway, Tyrrell County produced a full-color brochure that shows trails and roads and describes the area's history and points of interest. Copies of the brochure are distributed free at the highway rest stop.

*This boardwalk and greenway along the Scuppernong River in rural Tyrrell County, North Carolina, is the first step in the county's efforts to enhance its appeal to tourists; a state-of-the-art visitor center also is planned. Residents hope to capitalize on their proximity to more than 500,000 acres of pristine national wildlife refuges. (Page Crutcher, The Conservation Fund)*

If a region is to truly benefit from tourism, however, it needs more than just an attraction and a rest stop. It also needs an infrastructure to provide visitors with travel-related services like motels, bed and breakfasts, restaurants, shopping opportunities, bicycle and canoe rentals, fishing tackle, and so on. To help local people develop and operate these types of businesses, Tyrrell County created a new Community Development Corporation (CDC) to provide technical assistance, loans, and information. The CDC has established a job-training and placement program to help local 18- to 25-year-olds complete high school, find work, or enroll in college. Some of them helped build the greenway and boardwalk.

Tyrrell County also recognizes that unbridled development could detract from the region's quality of life. With assistance from the University of North Carolina, the CDC is preparing a comprehensive development plan for the county that identifies economic options compatible with the region's wetland environment.

Nearby communities are taking notice and are now working with Tyrrell County to develop three other interpretive centers, each focusing on a different aspect of eastern North Carolina's natural and cultural environment.

To identify job opportunities for local 18- to 25-year-olds, Tyrrell County leaders created a Youth Conservation Corps that employs teenagers and young adults in community service projects such as this boardwalk along the Scuppernong River. The group also provides opportunities for job training and higher education. (Page Crutcher, The Conservation Fund)

Together, the four centers will be the linchpins of a regionwide plan to promote tourism in the region. Spearheading the effort is a new group called the Partnership for the Sounds, a coalition of eastern Carolina's business leaders, conservation groups, residents, and national wildlife refuge officials.

Tyrrell County is proving what other gateway communities are just beginning to realize: Economic development and resource conservation are inextricably linked—one won't work without the other. Or as Mikki Sager of The Conservation Fund says: "This isn't just sustainable development. It's sustainable conservation."

---

## The Economic Benefits of Greenways

*Real Property Values.* Many studies demonstrate that parks, greenways, and trails increase nearby property values, which can enhance local tax revenues and help offset greenway acquisition costs.

*Expenditures by Residents.* Spending by local residents on greenway-related activities helps support recreation-oriented businesses and their employees, as well as other businesses that are patronized by greenway and trail users.

*Tourism.* Greenways are often tourist attractions that generate expenditures for food, lodging, and recreation-oriented services. Greenways also help improve the overall appeal of a community to prospective tourists and residents.

*Agency Expenditures.* The agency responsible for managing a river, trail, or greenway can help support local businesses by purchasing supplies and services. Jobs created by the managing agency can also add to local employment opportunities.

*Corporate Relocation.* Evidence shows that a community's quality of life is an increasingly important factor in corporate decisions about where to locate. Greenways are often cited as important contributors to quality of life.

*Public Cost Reduction.* The conservation of rivers, trails, and greenways can help local governments minimize the costs of flooding and other natural hazards.

Source: National Park Service: *The Economic Impacts of Protecting Rivers, Trails, and Greenway Corridors* (1994).

---

# Notes

page 23: More information on visitation to public lands is available from National Park Service, Statistics (WASO-TNT), P.O. Box 25287, Denver, Colorado 80225, phone: (303) 969-6977; U.S. Fish and Wildlife Service, Division of Refuges, 4401 N. Fairfax Drive, Mail Stop 670, Arlington, Virginia 22203, phone: (703) 358-2029; U.S. Forest Service, Recreation Staff, 4 Central Auditors Building, 201 14th Street, S.W., Washington, D.C. 20250, phone: (202) 205-1706.

**page 25:** For additional information on Branson, see "A Perfect American Town: Utopia, Missouri," *The Economist*, January 6, 1995, pp. 25–28.

**page 26:** Thanks to Ray Rasker for help in assembling the criteria by which communities can evaluate tourism development.

**page 27:** Additional data on the economic benefits of scenic byways are in *The Economic Impact of Travel on Scenic Byways*, 1990, by the U.S. Travel Data Center, an arm of the Federal Highway Administration, Washington, D.C. See also *The Economic Impacts of the Blue Ridge Parkway*, 1990, by the Southeastern Research Institute, Inc., Federal Highway Administration, Washington, D.C.

**page 28:** More details on wildlife-related tourism are in *The 1991 National Survey of Fishing, Hunting, and Wildlife-Associated Recreation*, by the U.S. Department of Commerce and U.S. Department of the Interior, U.S. Government Printing Office, Washington, D.C.

**page 29:** For information on the economics of bird-watching, see *The Economic Impact of Birding Ecotourism on Communities Surrounding Eight National Wildlife Refuges*, 1995, U.S. Fish and Wildlife Service, conducted by Dr. Paul Kerlinger. Also, obtain a copy of the *Directory of Birding Festivals* from the National Fish and Wildlife Foundation, 1120 Connecticut Avenue, N.W., Suite 900, Washington, D.C. 20036, phone: (202) 857-0166.

**page 30:** For more information on how Fredericksburg's historic preservation program has revitalized the local economy, see *The Economic Benefits of Preserving Community Character: A Case Study from Fredericksburg, Virginia*, 1991, by the Government Finance Research Center of the Government Finance Officers Association, Chicago.

**page 32:** For more information on Townsend and Pittman Center, contact Great Smoky Mountains National Park, Gatlinburg, Tennessee 37738, phone: (615) 436-1200; Southern Appalachian Man and Biosphere Program, 1314 Cherokee Orchard Road, Gatlinburg, Tennessee 37738, phone: (615) 436-7120. Also, see *The FutureScape of Pittman Center*, 1995, by the East Tennessee Community Design Center and the Tennessee Valley Authority.

**page 36:** For more information about Gettysburg, contact Gettysburg–Adams County Area Chamber of Commerce, 33 York Street, Gettysburg, Pennsylvania 17325, phone: (717) 334-8151; Gettysburg National Military Park, 97 Taneytown Road, Gettysburg, Pennsylvania 17325, phone: (717) 334-1124. Also, see *Gettysburg National Military Park and Eisenhower National Historic Site: Economic Impact on Gettysburg and Adams County*, 1994, by Matthew McAvoy, published by the Gettysburg–Adams County Chamber of Commerce.

**page 40:** For more information on Tyrrell County, North Carolina, contact Tyrrell County Community Development Corporation, P.O. Box 58, Columbia, North Carolina 27925, phone: (919) 796-0193; Pocosin Lakes National Wildlife Refuge, Route 1, Box 195-B, Creswell, North Carolina 27928, phone: (919) 797-4431; The Conservation Fund, P.O Box 374, Chapel Hill, North Carolina 27514, phone: (919) 967-2223. Also, see *Eco-Tourism in Tyrrell County: Opportunities, Constraints, and Ideas for Action*, 1993, by the Institute for Economic Development, Department of City and Regional Planning, University of North Carolina, Chapel Hill, North Carolina. County Administrator J. D. Brickhouse is quoted in "Columbia Seeks Refuge Center," *Wildlife in North Carolina* magazine, August 1991.

# Chapter 4

# The Secrets of Successful Communities

How are some gateway communities able to maintain local character and quality of life in the face of strong pressure for change, while others lose the very features that give them distinction and appeal? How can communities grow and prosper without compromising their character and surroundings?

From coast to coast, gateway communities are struggling to find answers to these questions. To help them, we visited dozens of communities throughout the country, meeting with county commissioners, public land managers, farmers, ranchers, city council members, conservationists, developers, chamber of commerce directors, land-use planners, and concerned citizens. We discovered that many gateway communities have found ways to retain their scenic beauty, small-town values, historic character, and sense of community, yet sustain a prosperous economy. And they've done it without accepting the runaway growth that transforms some communities into sprawling towns or tourist traps that no longer instill a sense of pride in residents.

Each of these "successful" communities differs from the next, but they all share some common characteristics. It's clear, for instance, that these communities actively involve a broad cross-section of residents in determining and planning for the future. They also capitalize on their distinctive assets—their architecture, history, and natural surroundings—rather than trying to adopt a new and different identity. Most successful gateway communities also utilize a variety of private-sector tools and market incentives to influence their design, instead of relying solely on regulations or government programs.

Not every successful gateway community displays all of the following characteristics, but most have made use of at least a few:

1. Develop a widely shared vision

2. Create an inventory of local resources

3. Build on local assets

4. Minimize the need for regulations

5. Meet the needs of both landowner and community

6. Team up with public land managers

7. Recognize the role of nongovernmental organizations

8. Provide opportunities for leaders to step forward

9. Pay attention to aesthetics

What follows are examples and case studies from gateway communities across the country for each of these characteristics—living proof that communities looking for answers don't have to start from scratch.

## Develop a Widely Shared Vision

*Where there is no vision the people will perish.*
—Proverbs 29:18

Every successful business, organization, or individual has a plan for the future. Communities are no different. If nothing else, a community needs to agree on a shared vision of what it wants to become. This vision should address the full range of local concerns: schools, housing, economic development, neighborhoods, parks and open space, and protection of traditional industries like farming, commercial fishing, logging, or ranching.

Creating a shared vision is important because it provides a blueprint for the future of the community. People may differ on how to achieve the community's vision, but without a blueprint nothing will happen.

The first step for any gateway community interested in producing a vision is to organize a town meeting or workshop where a broad cross-section of citizens participates in discussing the future of the community. For the process to work, community leaders must forego the conventional closed decision-making process in which a government commission or panel listens to an array of speakers and special interests and then makes an "objective" decision about the community's future. Instead, community leaders need to invest in a different process, one that delegates responsibility for decisions to partnerships that involve individual citizens in the community.

When people realize that they are responsible for finding solutions to a problem, they tend to become more flexible and less dogmatic in their own views. They begin to see issues from one another's perspective and arrive at a solution that, while perhaps not anyone's ideal outcome, is one that everyone in the community can live with. This process is particularly effective in gateway communities and other small towns where people tend to feel strongly about their neighborhoods, natural surroundings, and sense of community. Almost always, residents of gateway communities share more common ground than they realize.

Authentic public involvement in a "visioning" process takes more than just arranging a few meetings—it requires a firm commitment to inform, involve, and educate the public. Well-designed education and outreach programs are crucial: publicize the event in the local newspaper; post flyers

*Like any successful business or organization, a community needs to develop a vision for its future. Such a vision should integrate all of a community's priorities, from promoting a vibrant economy to protecting natural lands. Here, residents of Moab, Utah, discuss options for their future. (Liz Rosan)*

about it in churches, restaurants, public buildings; organize a phone tree to alert people.

To encourage the best possible turnout at a workshop, organizers should devise innovative ways to get people to attend, such as featuring a social hour or arranging for a popular speaker to address the group. Also, dates and times should be scheduled to accommodate working people, and on-site child care should be made available for parents.

Even then, the community may find it is missing a subset of people necessary for complete representation. If so, organizers should make extra efforts to involve those in the community who might be skeptical of a workshop centered around planning for the future. Sometimes just sitting down and talking with skeptics can resolve their concerns. Even if it doesn't, establishing a working dialogue can be a stepping stone to progress on other issues.

Once public participation is assured, organizers can turn their attention to the visioning process. A successful visioning process has three phases: In the first phase, community members identify the values and assets of their community. Small groups of participants sit down and discuss what makes their community an attractive and appealing place in which to live and work. These can include features like friendly neighbors, good schools, a vital downtown business district, or scenic views of mountains, valleys, and other landmarks. All input should be recognized and recorded. Trained facilitators can help.

In the second phase, these same teams articulate their preferred vision for the community's future. What do they want their community to look like in 5, 10, or 20 years? What kind of change is desirable? What kind of change is not desirable?

The final phase of the workshop is the most important. It's here where the groups identify the specific strategies and steps that will allow them to realize their vision. After each discussion group presents its workplan to the larger group, facilitators help all the participants prioritize their strategies and assume responsibilities and time frames for meeting them.

Some communities have found it effective to set aside the most divisive issues and focus on a smaller set of activities where there is broad agreement. Basing local programs on the highest shared interest can result in immediate progress, whereas trying to resolve thorny issues often leads to stalemate. Save those for later.

It's important for people to have ownership in the workplan that results from the visioning process, and just as important to delegate specific tasks and jobs—with time frames for accomplishing them—to workshop participants and other members of the community. To achieve results, regular follow-up meetings and updates on progress are essential.

A final report documenting what transpired at the workshop also is helpful. For example, what did participants say they valued most about the community? What kind of changes did they think were desirable? What were the elements of the community's vision for the future? What were some of the specific projects that citizens decided to undertake to realize their vision? A final report also helps to reinforce the sense of partnership and shared decision making fostered at the workshop. And it's something that can be continually referred to long after the workshop is over.

In some cases, the community may want to use the report to outline a course of action or list the steps that need to be undertaken to realize the vision. So that deadlines are met, time frames can be included as well. Some communities have even gone as far as including the names of people who agreed to accept responsibility for certain tasks or projects.

Here are a few examples of gateway communities that have used visioning processes as a tool to initiate local programs to keep their communities special:

• Ever since Lander, Wyoming, was rated the fifth-best small town in America in a guidebook for city dwellers looking to relocate to rural settings, people have been flocking to this community of about 7,500 people on the shoulders of the Wind River Range. Concerned that Lander's sudden popularity might overwhelm the community, the local chamber of commerce in 1994 organized a visioning process to give citizens a voice in determining the city's future. During the process, christened Lander Valley 2020, a disparate group of residents realized that (1) they cared a great deal about Lander's quality of life, and (2) they didn't want to lose it to the newest wave of growth. "Everything boils down to the same question," says Paula McCormick, president of the chamber of commerce. "How can we maintain our quality of life as we grow?" As a result of the workshop, several citizen-based task forces are busy working on the issues residents identified as most important: keeping agriculture and ranching viable, understanding and safeguarding water supplies, improving relations with the adjoining Wind River Indian Reservation, minimizing outdoor lighting, and informing the public about land-use tools that other communities have used successfully. "The common thread is the willingness to work together, to sit down and talk openly about things," McCormick says. Lander is now forming a new nonprofit organization that will be able to obtain grants and funding. "The community's decided what needs to be done," McCormick says. "Now we need the funds to carry out these activities."

• Ocracoke, North Carolina, is a small seaside community located on one of the narrow barrier islands that make up Cape Hatteras National

Seashore. Like many coastal communities, Ocracoke is a summer destination for many Americans. In 1991, residents became concerned that growth had reached the point where it was no longer a benefit to their community. A series of meetings on the community's future was held. To encourage public participation, a local county commissioner appointed a citizens advisory committee that sent every resident a flyer announcing the series; local newspapers also ran articles and ads promoting the event. The vision statement that resulted seeks to prevent Ocracoke from becoming a resort island unaffordable to residents. The community has barred new marinas, limited development of coastal wetlands, and prohibited construction of a sewage treatment plant (which residents felt would spur over-development). Ocracoke's vision succeeded in part because proponents of managing growth persuaded a broad cross-section of island residents to participate in the planning process.

• Springhill, Montana, is a small community of about 50 farms and ranches located on the western slope of the Bridger Range. When growth in nearby Bozeman resulted in proposals to subdivide several local ranches, Springhill found itself without any means of protecting its agricultural land and rural way of life. In 1991, local landowners responded by creating a citizens committee charged with listening to what residents wanted for the future and providing options. "We found that people were comfortable with the current rate of growth of one or two houses a year since 1960," says member Randy Johnson. "But they wanted to maintain the rural atmosphere and keep farmers farming." To achieve the community's goals, the citizens committee proposed a zoning ordinance that allows one house per 160 acres but permits additional residential development if the landowner agrees to a public hearing on the proposal and commits to keeping 85 percent of his or her entire property as agricultural land or open space.

• In Chattanooga, Tennessee, a visioning process conducted in 1984 attracted more than 1,700 people and identified 40 goals for the city to pursue, including making better use of the Tennessee River waterfront, converting municipal buses to electric power, creating a shelter for victims of domestic violence, and renovating two theaters. Vision 2000 was one of the first community-wide goal-setting processes in the country. It's also been one of the most successful. A follow-up survey conducted in 1992 found that Chattanooga had accomplished 85 percent of its Vision 2000 goals. One of the most popular projects to arise from Vision 2000 was the Tennessee Riverpark, a 20-mile greenway along the river. Designed to make Chattanooga's riverfront more accessible, the Riverpark boasts an all-

In a visioning process conducted in 1984, residents of Chattanooga, Tennessee, recommended that the city make better use of its waterfront on the Tennessee River. The result was Riverpark, a 20-mile-long walkway with picnic facilities, pedestrian bridges, and fishing piers like this one. (RiverValley Partners)

weather walkway, fishing piers, pedestrian bridges across the river, and picnic facilities. The Riverpark alone has stimulated more than a quarter of a billion dollars of new downtown development, including a highly acclaimed freshwater aquarium.

• In Arizona's San Rafael Valley, a 90,000-acre stretch of rolling grasslands bounded by the Coronado National Forest and the U.S.–Mexico border, ranchers set aside their chores for a few days in 1994 to work out a shared vision for the valley's future. After identifying what they valued about their lifestyle in the valley, participants then discussed strategies that could protect those values from residential subdivision. The resulting vision statement is now guiding local actions to preserve the valley's rural character, open space, and ranching lifestyle. In 1995, residents created the San Rafael Valley Land Trust, which helps ranchers protect their homesteads from residential development. The land trust already has been given a conservation easement on 450 acres of ranchland and is informing other landowners of their conservation options.

Case Study
=====

# Jackson Hole, Wyoming

*Before a community can take control of its future, it first needs to involve citizens in deciding what it wants to be. In Jackson Hole, residents found that despite their varied backgrounds, they all loved Jackson's mountain views, wildlife, and outdoor opportunities. And they all recognized that double-digit growth threatens what they cherish. Jackson citizens used this common ground to forge a shared vision for the future that establishes goals and strategies for securing affordable housing, protecting wildlife, and preserving views and open space. That vision is now guiding local decision making.*

The granite crags of Wyoming's Teton Range may be the most famous peaks in the United States. Ansel Adams found them irresistible. So too did John D. Rockefeller, Jr., who bought up nearly all the private ranches in their eastern shadow—about 114,000 acres in all—and donated the entire package to the National Park Service.

Stretching out beneath the Tetons' steep eastern face lies Jackson Hole, a high-elevation valley 50 miles long and, at its widest, 10 miles across . The northern end of the valley borders Yellowstone National Park, Grand Teton National Park makes up its middle, and at the valley's southern terminus— at 6,200 feet above sea level—is the town of Jackson, a thriving community of about 5,000 people.

Incorporated in 1914, Jackson has long been a popular destination for tourists on their way to the two national parks, the nearby wilderness areas, and the National Elk Refuge, one of the nation's most popular national wildlife refuges. During the summer, as many as 60,000 people a day pass through the town.

Jackson has developed a bustling economy dependent on tourism. Visitors can enjoy whitewater rafting or fishing trips down the Snake River, dude ranching, shopping in posh boutiques and art galleries in the town square, dining at five-star restaurants with Dom Perignon and chateaubriand, or downhill skiing at a resort with the biggest vertical drop (4,100 feet) of any ski area in the country. This isn't your traditional western economy.

Many visitors to Jackson Hole like the area so much they decide to stay. Some move here permanently, others build second homes. Teton County's population doubled in the 1970s and grew by more than 25 percent in the 1980s. "For decades, the only bulldozer in Jackson Hole belonged to the Forest Service," says Gene Hoffman, whose family has lived in Jackson Hole for four generations. "I think it's safe to say that era has ended."

Some newcomers build what resident Ben Read calls "trophy homes," huge houses of 10,000, 15,000, even 20,000 square feet. "Trophies here are

*The National Elk Refuge in Jackson Hole, Wyoming, provides wintering habitat for nearly 10,000 elk. Subdivision of open land, however, has sealed off important migration routes that the elk need to reach the refuge. A visioning exercise in 1990 helped Jackson Hole residents find ways to preserve the community's wildlife, mountain views, and economic diversity. (Kevin Painter, National Elk Refuge)*

no longer measured in points on a rack," he says, "but in bedrooms and square feet." Trophy-home builders hail from zip codes all over the country: Jet-setters from Miami, Hollywood, and Manhattan all spend part of the year in Jackson.

The region's growth, however, is changing what people love about Jackson Hole. Downtown Jackson, for example, now resembles an upscale shopping mall. Gone are many of the original stores, cafes, and restaurants. "Our local mom-and-pop retail is about to become a thing of the past," says County Commissioner Sandy Shuptrine. "We're almost totally outlet stores now."

Wildlife stand to lose the most from development. Although 97 percent of Teton County is in public ownership, the private lands in the county are critical to the area's wildlife. Settlers to the area homesteaded on the rich and fertile bottomlands in the valley, where winters are mildest and grazing is best. These are the same lands that provide wintering grounds for 80 percent of the greater Yellowstone ecosystem's endangered trumpeter swans, 43 percent of its moose, 41 percent of its bald eagles, and 40 percent of its mule deer.

The demand for second homes also has made it difficult for longtime residents to continue to afford to live here. Over the last 15 years, land and housing prices have tripled, forcing more than a quarter of the area's workforce to commute from neighboring communities. In 1994, the average price of a single-family home was $255,000; more than half the county's housing starts are seasonal or second homes. A recent study by the county concluded that "the current housing situation is creating a layered, horizontal social structure" due to the proliferation of exclusive subdivisions and "the inability of many growing, young families to afford a permanent home."

In 1995, Teton County and Jackson both adopted new land-use plans that seek to preserve Jackson Hole's natural resources and community character. The plans grew out of a public workshop five years earlier that sought to unite residents behind a shared vision for the region's future. More than 300 residents—representing the entire spectrum of views in the county—joined together to consider the future of Jackson Hole. The workshop was sponsored by 47 organizations, ranging from local environmental groups to the chamber of commerce. "It worked because the impetus came from the community," says Pam Lichtman, a local environmental advocate.

Despite their differences, participants soon realized they shared the same feelings about Jackson Hole's small-town flavor, beautiful scenery, abundant wildlife, and outdoor opportunities. And they decided the most pressing need was for Teton County and Jackson to jointly develop a new land-use plan to protect these assets.

The new plan, which was adopted in 1995, combines local regulations with financial incentives that give landowners sound reasons to conserve their property. Under the county's new zoning code, for example, the minimum lot size in rural areas is 35 acres, a big change from the 3- and 6-acre zoning in place before the plan took effect. But if landowners agree to cluster development and set aside part of their property as open space, the county offers a bonus that increases the density to between two and six homes per 35 acres. (The actual density depends on the size of the property being developed and the percentage of it set aside as open space.) The undeveloped portion of the property remains in private ownership but is permanently protected as agricultural land or open space. The density bonus already has resulted in the protection of more than 1,500 acres, as well as in more efficient land development patterns.

Teton County also identified 26,000 acres of land crucial to the well-being of its native wildlife; before any development can proceed in these areas, the county and the developer are required to prepare a detailed analysis of how the project will affect wildlife. Wildlife also will benefit from new standards that require fencing to be of the "wildlife-friendly" post-and-pole construction.

In the same manner, the county designated a number of scenic areas in which development must meet design standards intended to preserve views of the Tetons or Snake River corridor. In these predesignated areas, the location, size, height, and color of a building must not impinge on scenery.

Because residents identified the rising cost of housing as one of their chief concerns, the plan requires that at least 15 percent of the housing built in new subdivisions be affordable to people earning less than 120 percent of the county's median income. It also imposes an impact fee on expensive new homes, with the revenue used to subsidize affordable housing. The amount of the fee is determined by the size of the home being built. Homes 3,100 square feet or larger, for example, are assessed a $2,240 fee, while homes 1,900 square feet or smaller pay nothing. Finally, to limit construction of the trophy homes that have driven up property values and created eyesores on many a ridge line, homes larger than 8,000 square feet no longer will be permitted in the county.

The plan is by no means the final word in the debate over land use in Teton County. Many residents wish it were more aggressive, others say it places too many restrictions on land development. Nearly everyone, however, agrees that the plan represents an important step to finding a shared approach to protecting the world-class resources of Jackson Hole.

## Create an Inventory of Local Resources

*If you don't know the ground, you're probably wrong about everything else.*
—Norman Maclean

An accurate, concise profile of a community's natural and man-made resources, demographics, and economic trends is the starting point of any land-use or community-development initiative. Before citizens can make informed decisions about their future, they need to know the status of all the factors relevant to preparing for change. A citizens committee can be chartered to conduct this inventory. Depending on the community's fiscal situation, a consultant may also be hired. Gateway communities also might want to make use of the wealth of resources available from the park, refuge, or natural area on their borders.

Start with the simple things: Maps that identify land ownership are always helpful. How many acres are privately owned? What is the existing zoning? What will the community look like if developed at the level allowed in the zoning ordinances?

Gateway communities also need to consider public lands. How many acres are in public ownership? What activities are permitted on those lands? What are the agency's future plans?

*Before citizens can make informed decisions about their future, they need to know the status of all the factors relevant to preparing for change. Here, a local planning committee reviews maps of a proposed project. (David Church)*

Local history is important, too. Not only is it of interest to most residents, it's also a major element in determining the community's future directions. Moreover, interviewing longtime residents about the community's past is a good way to get them interested and invested in an initiative.

Local demographics and land-use trends are also useful. Is the community growing? Where is the growth occurring? What are recent trends in subdivision and building permits? What areas are best suited to supporting new growth? What are the income and age characteristics of the population? Is housing remaining affordable to residents?

Information on natural resources is vital. What are the soil and vegetation types in the area? Are there endangered species? What are the surface and groundwater conditions? Maps of these resources can help people interpret and understand often complicated information.

Economic data and trends also should be included. What are the principal sources of local jobs and income? Which industries or sectors are growing? Which are declining? What's happening to the economy at the regional level?

Finally, a review of local land-use ordinances, state and federal mandates, and the community's existing master plan—if there is one—can help residents understand the legal requirements their activities must comply with.

Here are a few examples of communities that have used inventories to launch effective local land-use initiatives:

• Hot Springs, North Carolina, is one of only a few towns located directly on the Appalachian Trail, the nation's first interstate recreational trail. After an out-of-town investor developed a resort amid the hot mineral springs for which the town is named, the town council quickly appointed a citizens committee to examine the town's options for dealing with an expected growth spurt. The committee decided that before it could take any action, it needed information about the town's natural and cultural assets. The committee surveyed residents and held five public forums to identify Hot Springs's important scenic, historic, and cultural resources. The resulting inventory provided the basis for an informed discussion of the town's future. Residents of Hot Springs also established a nonprofit group, the Hot Springs Horizons Project, to work closely with the town council on zoning matters, economic renewal projects, and downtown beautification.

• In Maryville, Tennessee, a gateway to Great Smoky Mountains National Park, residents concerned with rapid development of the farms and foothills in the park's western fringe established a land trust to protect the area's scenery and character. The first task of the Foothills Land Conservancy was to inventory the lands surrounding the park to identify priorities for protection. With help from the geography department at the University of Tennessee, the conservancy produced a series of maps documenting prime agricultural soils, scenic vistas, and wildlife habitat and migration corridors. The maps not only helped the conservancy identify the most critical tracts, they also demonstrated to the public the importance of conserving valuable lands. Since 1992, the conservancy has protected more than 6,000 acres of land.

• Located on a fragile barrier island, Nags Head, North Carolina, is a gateway to Pea Island National Wildlife Refuge and Cape Hatteras National Seashore. While Nags Head's year-round population numbers only 2,000 people, its summer population swells to more than 40,000. Concerns about water—citizens get their drinking water from an aquifer under the island— prompted the town to adopt several strategies to manage growth. Nags Head began by identifying the number of people it could support after taking into account the town's water supply, sewer capacity, and amount of developable land. "We needed to find out what were the most limiting factors," says Mayor Donald Bryan. The resulting information helped channel growth to the areas best suited for development, shunting it from aquifer-recharge zones, wetlands, and areas most susceptible to flooding, erosion, and hurricane damage.

• Breckenridge, Colorado, bordered on three sides by the White River National Forest, is perhaps best known for the downhill-ski resort of the same name. When the resort expanded in 1978, Breckenridge initiated a comprehensive planning process that began with an inventory of its historic buildings, a detailed analysis of natural resources, and a survey to determine which issues citizens believed most important to the town's future. The town then adopted a performance-based development code that rates projects on factors such as architectural compatibility, open-space conservation, landscaping, affordable housing, and water and energy conservation. To win approval, a project must not only score a certain number of points but also meet several minimum criteria.

Case Study
===
## Sanibel Island, Florida

*Many gateway communities face daunting growth pressures that threaten their most treasured assets. In Sanibel Island, residents made sure that a soaring demand for seaside resorts and beach houses didn't come at the expense of their white-sand beaches, bird life, and quiet charm. To determine an appropriate level of development, Sanibel bases its master plan on what's needed to protect the island's wildlife and natural systems. Understanding its ecological limits helps Sanibel prosper in a way that respects its fragile coastal environment.*

Sanibel Island is one of a string of barrier islands that encircles Florida like a delicate necklace. Located on the Gulf Coast, just off the mainland from Fort Myers, Sanibel extends over an area 12 miles long and three miles wide. More than 6,000 people live here year-round.

Sanibel's white-sand beaches and crystal-clear waters have been attracting vacationers for decades; in 1994, more than one million people visited the Island. Sanibel also is one of the world's premier places to collect seashells. The Island's east–west configuration makes it a natural depository for shells churned up by currents that flow north along the coast.

Synonymous with Sanibel is the J.N. "Ding" Darling National Wildlife Refuge. Set aside in 1945, Ding Darling occupies nearly half the island. Its 5,300 acres of tropical hardwoods, beaches, freshwater marshes, and mangrove islands provide nesting sites for more than 250 species of birds, including the American avocet, brown pelican, osprey, and roseate spoonbill, as well as egrets and herons of all shapes and sizes. It is also home to over 50 types of reptiles, including alligators, sea turtles, and the endangered American crocodile.

*Sanibel Island, Florida, has found ways to protect its fragile coastal environment from the impacts of more than a million visitors a year. Underlying Sanibel's success at growth management is a solid understanding of the island's ecological limits. (Ed McMahon)*

What makes Sanibel unique among gateway communities is its reliance on ecological constraints to establish boundaries and standards for development. In doing so, Sanibel has managed to preserve one of America's most exceptional subtropical wildlife habitats while also accommodating a high level of visitation.

Sanibel's encounter with growth began in earnest in 1963, when Lee County completed a three-mile causeway that links the island with the mainland. Before that, visitors to Sanibel came and went by boat or ferry. With the causeway making the island easily accessible, Sanibel quickly became a magnet for development. (Even today, residents refer fondly to the quieter days before the causeway's construction as B.C.—before causeway.)

Shortly after the causeway's opening, a consortium of resort developers successfully sued to overturn Sanibel's independent zoning authority, stripping residents of their control over land-use decisions on the island. That left decisions with the Lee County Board of Commissioners, who classified the island as though it were any mainland area suitable for intensive development. By permitting condominiums on sand dunes and golf courses in wetlands, the county would have allowed Sanibel's population to soar to more than 90,000 (currently, the peak season population is about 15,000). A four-lane expressway was even planned through the heart of the wildlife refuge.

In 1974, however, the citizens of Sanibel, frustrated with a county government that ignored the island's unique characteristics, took matters into their own hands and voted to incorporate as the City of Sanibel. Within a few weeks of incorporation, a new city government had begun work on a plan to conserve Sanibel's remarkable assets and quality of life: its beaches, mangrove swamps, drinking water, and wildlife.

The city council's first task was to impose a moratorium on all new development; it then hired environmental planners to conduct a detailed inventory of the island's natural resources. Based on this analysis, which became known as *The Sanibel Report*, Sanibel in 1976 enacted a comprehensive land-use plan that allows continued development yet takes steps to protect the island's natural resources.

The original plan had five major features. First, it set a limit on Sanibel's population consistent with the need to evacuate the island before hurricanes. The narrow causeway restricts the flow of traffic from the island, thereby imposing a ceiling on population. A shortage of drinking water on the island also limits the city's size; heavy demand for water would quickly contaminate the island's groundwater aquifers with seawater.

Second, the plan shunted development away from wetlands, sand dunes, beaches, and other sensitive areas. An additional 2,000 structures (beyond 1976 levels) were approved, but only in areas capable of supporting development.

Third, the plan established for all development strong performance standards, which vary depending on the ecological "zone" in which a project lies. Six zones were established: Gulf beach, bay beach, Gulf beach ridge, interior wetland basin, mid-island ridge, and mangrove. Some standards apply across the board—for example, no billboards or buildings taller than four stories are permitted. And not only do all commercial buildings and parking lots require lush landscaping, the city mandates the use of native plants and prohibits removal of vegetation that contributes to beach stability.

Fourth, the plan sought to restore areas that had suffered ecological damage. Beach dunes have been replanted with native vegetation, drainage systems removed from wetlands, and mangrove swamps replenished with water.

Fifth, the plan took steps to involve the public in determining and realizing the island's future. Before the city issues a building permit, for example, a citizens committee investigates the site and works with the developer to retain as many native trees as possible. Significant trees that can't be saved are transplanted to other sites.

Many individuals and groups contributed to the plan, but the key organization supporting the process was the Sanibel-Captiva Conservation Foundation. Founded in 1967, this citizens group works closely with the city to preserve the natural resources on Sanibel Island and its smaller sister island to the north, Captiva Island. Today, the organization has 9 full-time staff members, 300 volunteers, and 2,500 members.

The foundation owns more than 1,000 acres of land, mostly along the Sanibel River corridor, which it jointly manages with the city. It conducts regular beach cleanups and habitat management and restoration projects, and it closely monitors development proposals on both islands, as well as activities at all levels of government. The foundation's programs are tightly linked to the goals of the city's land-use plan. An example is the foundation's native-plant nursery, which provides developers and homeowners with the vegetation necessary to meet the city's building code. On-site consultation is available on everything from caring for native plants to choosing plants that will attract wildlife.

Environmental education is a large part of the group's mission. In 1991, the foundation produced a series of short educational films designed to inform visitors and tourists of ways to enjoy their visit to Sanibel without affecting wildlife or habitat. The films cover a range of topics, including the danger of feeding alligators, Florida's laws on collecting sand dollars and live shells, and the impact of littering and speeding. The films are broadcast four times an hour on Visitor's Television, better known as VTV, a local cable television station created specifically to provide information for tourists on the day's activities. Each film is aired along with spots about Sanibel's restaurants, entertainment and night life, and upcoming events and activities. It's a popular channel among vacationers interested in learning about the day's activities.

Today, 20 years after the adoption of the land-use plan, Sanibel is a success story. Its homes and businesses are adorned with lush native landscaping, and its streets are lined with a thick canopy of trees. Unlike most communities on the Florida coast, there are no high rises, billboards, or gaudy signs. Everywhere, bicyclists can be seen pedaling to work or to the beach on an extensive network of paved bike trails.

At Ding Darling National Wildlife Refuge, a state-of-the-art educational center and bookstore welcome visitors. After a brief orientation at the center, most visitors head for Wildlife Drive, a five-mile, one-way loop that provides a self-guided tour of the refuge. To cope with the impact of 750,000 visitors a year, the refuge has banned trucks, commercial buses, and mopeds and set up a popular tram transportation system. Other visitors head for Tarpon Bay, where a concessionaire rents canoes, kayaks, and bicycles. (Motor boats are prohibited because of their potential to disturb the refuge's wildlife.)

"We have two basic options," says Ranger Steve Alvarez. "Restrict use or educate people on how to better use the refuge. We'd rather educate visitors."

The combined impact of residential and resort development and a million visitors a year is extensive. But by using ecological information to establish parameters for land use, and by working in partnership with the city, private groups, and the U.S. Fish and Wildlife Service, Sanibel Island has set a standard for balancing nature and commerce in a fragile coastal environment.

## Build on Local Assets

Successful gateway communities craft economic- and community-development policies around their distinctive assets: river corridors or waterfronts, stunning views of a mountain range or valley, a particular crop or manufactured product, a unique cultural heritage, a blue-ribbon trout stream, historic architecture, or unusual species of vegetation or wildlife.

Building on distinctive local assets is important for a number of reasons, according to land-use expert Chris Duerksen. First, these assets provide people with "a sense of place," a quality for which more and more Americans are searching. In an increasingly homogeneous society, a community with its own feel and flavor stands out. Second, distinctive assets enhance quality of life and thus can translate into economic vitality because of their power to attract and retain businesses, residents, and tourists. Many communities underestimate the link between quality of life and the local economy. And, finally, says Duerksen, "distinctive assets provide a focal point to generate political support and excitement for initiatives to protect what residents value." Most people understand the importance of protecting a river corridor, a wintering area for elk, a historic building, or a beautiful view of a mountain range or valley.

Gateway communities are unique in that their proximity to public lands gives them a distinctive asset that most communities lack. Gateway communities that base economic development strategies on their natural or historic assets also don't have to undergo expensive facelifts to stay abreast of ever-changing trends. They're not dependent on what's chic in American pop culture.

Here are just a few examples of how gateway communities have used local assets to help strengthen their economy and enhance their quality of life:

• Jackson, New Hampshire, is a gateway to the White Mountains of the state's north country. Jackson's most distinctive asset is Wildcat Brook, a clear, fast-flowing stream with a 165-foot waterfall, Jackson Falls, in the center of the village. In 1983, hydropower interests proposed to harness the stream's powerful current. Not wanting to see Wildcat Brook dammed, Jackson residents created a citizens committee to develop a comprehensive protection plan for the stream. The committee began by surveying residents and finding strong local support for protecting the river. Next, they commissioned a review of existing conservation measures. Deciding that further action was warranted, the committee developed a strategy to protect the river. They began by encouraging landowners along the stream to donate conservation easements on their property; 10 easements totaling 431 acres were donated. But the committee also persuaded the town council to require 75-foot setbacks for development along the stream and to base zoning density on soil septic capacity. Finally, the committee helped improve public access to the waterfall. In 1988, the citizens of Jackson convinced Congress to designate Wildcat Brook as a federally protected wild and scenic river, permanently barring hydropower development.

• A storied past is the principal asset of Manteo, North Carolina: The town was the site of the first English settlement in America, the ill-fated "Lost Colony" of 1587. Manteo also is a gateway to three national wildlife refuges and to Cape Hatteras National Seashore. Manteo's interest in its future was triggered not by tourism or rapid growth but by plans to commemorate the 400th anniversary of the colony. The town decided to use the event to galvanize support for long-term preservation of its image and identity. With assistance from North Carolina State University, Manteo solicited views from a wide cross-section of the community. It decided on a low-key tourism program emphasizing the town's history and waterfront. Downtown streets are now lined with shops and a new inn, billboards have been removed, and a replica of an Elizabethan-era frigate is anchored in the harbor.

• Wyoming is a leader in efforts to capitalize on the growing interest in observing wildlife. In 1987, the state launched a campaign—Wyoming's Wildlife: Worth the Watching—to market its wildlife-viewing opportunities. Highway overlooks, information kiosks, and visitor centers were built near prime wildlife-viewing sites. The state also developed a logo for the program, which is advertised in travel magazines, brochures, and on road signs. "Wildlife has always been one of Wyoming's biggest drawing cards," says Larry Kruckenberg of the state Game & Fish Department. The program's success in attracting tourists convinced dozens of towns in the state to incorporate the Worth the Watching logo into their tourism and business promotion. The result: substantial increases in tourism throughout the state and more diverse local economies. The Game & Fish Department estimates that wildlife-related activities generate $1 billion a year for the state's economy.

*To help local communities capture more of the tourism dollar, Wyoming created a logo to help visitors locate prime wildlife viewing areas throughout the state. (Ed McMahon)*

• Front Royal, Virginia, was long viewed as just a town to drive through on the way to Shenandoah National Park. Today, the town is a destination in and of itself. Capitalizing on its location next to the park, Front Royal recently completed the first phase of a network of bicycle trails and footpaths linking its downtown with "Skyline Drive," a popular two-lane byway through the park and the northern-most segment of the Blue Ridge Parkway. After a ride in the park, bicyclists are able to enjoy local restaurants, hotels, and shopping. The city also planted shade trees along all its major roads and invested in a public arts program that helped pay for outdoor murals on walls and buildings. Front Royal joins hundreds of gateway communities throughout the nation that are making use of old canal paths, abandoned railroad lines, river corridors—even power-line rights-of-way—to create trail corridors and greenways connecting natural areas, historic sites, and downtown commercial areas.

• Schuylerville, New York, is a gateway to Saratoga National Historical Park. In 1777, an army of Minutemen routed a British invasion force here in what many say marked the turning point of the Revolutionary War. Schuylerville went through some hard times in the 1970s when a paper mill left town but today is rebuilding its image and economy based on its rich history and Hudson River waterfront. "We're turning things around by capitalizing on Schuylerville's tremendous assets," says Mayor Kim Gamache. "Not many communities have a history or riverfront like ours." Schuylerville has erected road signs that direct visitors to historic sites in the village and built a visitor center to provide information on local points of interest. The village also secured $250,000 in federal transportation dollars to build a network of trails and historic markers along the Hudson. A picnic area already is in place and a public boat launch is planned. Schuylerville also has spruced up its downtown; in the summer, village merchants dress up the streets with life-size cutouts of Revolutionary War soldiers. New businesses, including a bait-and-tackle shop, an antique dealer, and even a gourmet potato chip maker, have sprung up. "We've still got some empty storefronts," says Gamache, "but there's a lot more activity now."

What about communities that lack an association with a famous natural or historic area— how can they develop a distinctive economy if they have no obvious assets? Many communities simply may not recognize the potential of the resources they have at hand.

• Butte, Montana, once the nation's leading producer of copper, received national historic landmark status in 1962. Evidence of the city's past still dominates the local landscape: Butte is riddled with abandoned mine shafts, open pit mines, slag heaps, and old buildings and warehouses. Once thought to be a liability, Butte's mining infrastructure is now the centerpiece of an economic revitalization strategy based on its mining heritage. The town is converting abandoned mine sites into community facilities and developing historical programs for residents and visitors. In the works are a smelting interpretive center, a greenway along a once-contaminated river, a "down-in-the-mine" tour, and audio tapes that guide visitors to the town's attractions and history. Atop an old dump in nearby Anaconda, Jack Nicklaus has even designed a golf course featuring sand traps made of the black slag left over from copper smelting.

• Lowell, Massachusetts, was the birthplace of the American industrial revolution and the site of the country's earliest experiments with assembly lines and automation. Lowell suffered a wrenching recession in the 1960s and 1970s as one by one its textile factories left town. Many people, however, including former Massachusetts senator Paul Tsongas, saw Lowell's abandoned mills as an asset. In 1978, Tsongas helped Lowell receive federal designation as a National Historical Park. With assistance from the National Park Service, Lowell used its industrial heritage to fashion an economy based on tourism and historic preservation. The city's downtown is now enjoying a renaissance as a center for offices and businesses, with old factories and warehouses converted to hotels, apartments, stores, and office space.

## Case Study

## Dubois, Wyoming

*Like people, communities often find they have unique strengths. When a local sawmill closed its doors in 1988, residents of frontier-town Dubois quickly organized a public workshop to determine how they could rebound from the loss of their largest employer. The group decided that rather than try to attract a new industry, Dubois needed to diversify its economy in a way that leveraged its most abundant assets—wildlife and wild lands. Today, the Dubois economy is a healthy mix of ranchers, hunting and fishing guides, wilderness outfitters, tourism-oriented businesses, and entrepreneurs who have relocated to the area because of its scenery and recreational lands.*

The Wind River begins high in the mountains of western Wyoming then races down the narrow valley it has cut between the Absaroka Mountains and the Wind River Range. Nestled between the two ranges, at 6,900 feet above sea level, sits Dubois, a town of about 900 people.

Dubois prides itself on its abundant wildlife. Just to the south is Whiskey Mountain, home to the largest concentration of bighorn sheep in the continental United States—more than a thousand animals. Elk, mule deer, pronghorn antelope, moose, mountain lions, and grizzly and black bears also inhabit the mountains and valleys around the town. A few years ago, in an effort to attract customers, a car-wash owner in Dubois attached a statue of a giant moose to the roof of his business. The wildlife theme caught on, and several larger-than-life statues of wildlife now grace the town: A bear guards the entrance to one motel, while an elk dominates the lawn of another; a 10-foot-long rainbow trout curls around a fishing pole outside the local tackle shop.

Even the restaurants cater to the outdoors enthusiast. Catch a few trout in the Wind River, and the Cowboy Cafe, a Main Street diner, will cook them up—cleaned in advance, please—and serve them to you with a baked potato and a vegetable for $4.50. (Don't leave without trying a slice of their homemade pie.)

Dubois at one time was a logging town with more than a third of its residents employed at a Louisiana–Pacific sawmill. When the mill shut down in 1988, many residents feared Dubois would become a ghost town.

*After a sawmill left town in 1988, Dubois, Wyoming, decided to rebuild its econo-*
*my based on its most important assets—wildlife and wild lands. Several wildlife*
*statues, including this moose, adorn the town. (Luther Propst)*

Dubois proved them wrong. Today, its economy is a diverse blend of Main
Street shops, hunting and fishing guides, motels, ranchers, custom furniture
manufacturers, wilderness outfitters, bed and breakfasts, retirees with pen-
sion and investment income, and log-home builders. Dubois also is attracting international consultants who report to work via the fax machine or computer modem, and who locate in Dubois because of the area's scenic setting
and outdoor opportunities.

The mill's closing may have actually helped Dubois by forcing residents
to prepare for the future. "After the mill left, we quickly realized that wild
lands and wildlife are our two most powerful and valuable resources," says
Pat Neary, a Dubois resident and director of the Fremont County Economic
Development Council. "The Dubois economy depends on their protection."
So much so that a few years after the sawmill closed, the Dubois Chamber
of Commerce shocked the U.S. Forest Service by opposing its decision to
expand oil and gas leasing in the nearby Shoshone National Forest. Because
of the chamber's protest, the agency scaled back leasing in the forest.

In 1993, Dubois received a significant economic boost with the opening
of the National Bighorn Sheep Center, a cooperative project financed by
Dubois residents, federal and state agencies, conservation organizations,
and local economic development groups. "The Town of Dubois has focused
its community development efforts on its most unique natural resource,"

reads a plaque in the center, "the Rocky Mountain bighorn sheep of Whiskey Mountain."

The center, which highlights the ecology of the Rocky Mountain bighorn sheep, isn't just a tourist attraction. It also operates educational programs for school children and conducts scientific studies of the local sheep population. In addition, the center's downtown location has sparked a new wave of investment on Dubois's Main Street.

Dubois is not without its problems, however. Like many other small, Rocky Mountain communities, Dubois is experiencing an influx of newcomers in search of small-town values and beautiful scenery.

In 1992, Dubois sponsored a community visioning workshop to give residents a stronger voice in the town's future. Posters announcing the workshop featured the long arm of a rhinestone-studded cowboy reaching over Togwotee Pass, a 9,984-foot-high gap in the Absaroka Range, which separates the Wind River valley from its upscale neighbor, Jackson Hole. "The rallying cry in Dubois was, 'We don't want to be like Jackson,'" says Mary Ellen Honsaker, a local artist.

The workshop attracted more than 120 people. "There was a tremendous

*Dubois boasts the largest bighorn sheep population in the Lower 48. A new museum highlighting the bighorn has helped stimulate increased investment in downtown Dubois. (National Bighorn Sheep Center)*

amount of involvement from all cross-sections of the community," Honsaker says. "We called every single person in the phone book to invite them to help determine the future of Dubois." Residents found they shared many of the same opinions about the town. Above all, they liked Dubois because, in the words of Honsaker, "It's a real town. Cowboys come here to shop for gear— there aren't any tourist traps."

After the workshop, Dubois residents formed citizens committees to work toward the goals they drew up. One of their first projects was a down-town beautification campaign. More than 100 people helped plant trees along Main Street. "We started with easy projects to show the benefits of staying together and having common goals to work toward," says Honsaker.

Other citizens committees have tackled issues such as architectural guidelines for homes and businesses, affordable housing, and land use plan-ning. One committee received an $8,000 grant to map the most important wildlife habitat in the region.

The key to Dubois's success may lie in its refusal to follow the traditional economic development textbook for rural communities, which calls for lay-ing out the welcome mat to any industry or development that chances by. Instead, Dubois is trying to find economic opportunities that allow it to build on its existing assets. "You can put up a front to attract people," says Mary Ellen Honsaker, "or you can tell your own story."

## Minimize the Need for Regulations

Successful gateway communities don't rely solely on local government reg-ulations to ensure that development meets their needs and desires. To be sure, local land-use regulations and ordinances are essential in establishing a minimum code of conduct and preventing the worst in development. They can keep development out of floodplains, minimize soil erosion from steep slopes, and bar commercial expansion into neighborhoods. By themselves, however, regulations will not bring out the best in a community or protect what people value most about their town. Because they focus on prevention, regulations cannot offer a positive vision of how things should be. Without other approaches, communities might well experience indistinguishable, look-alike development that simply follows the letter of the law.

Initiatives that rely exclusively on regulations also tend to have a short life. Often, a county commission or city council will enact tough regulations only to see them repealed or weakened by a future commission or council with different ideas.

If regulations aren't the entire answer, how can gateway communities en-sure that development meets local needs? Successful gateway communities have found a variety of creative ways to influence the development process: innovative programs to acquire sensitive lands, tax abatements that promote the rehabilitation of historic buildings, incentives that encourage developers to plan projects with the needs of the larger community in mind, or educational campaigns that encourage voluntary action by citizens. Communities couple these tools and market incentives with sound, widely accepted regulations. The result is a balanced approach that offers a variety of ways to meet local goals. This strategy works especially well when there is no local consensus on a regulatory program or land-use goal.

Here are a few examples:

• Tax incentives are highly effective at spurring the business sector. In Fredericksburg, Virginia, the site of four Civil War battles, property owners who renovate historic buildings are granted a seven-year grace period from increases in property taxes. The program, which has been in place since 1981, applies to any property located within the city's historic district. The tax savings are substantial enough that local developers actively search for abandoned historic buildings to convert to new uses. "It's been instrumental in encouraging redevelopment downtown," says Eric Nelson of Fredericksburg's planning office. More than 250 buildings have been restored under the program.

• Reno, Nevada, isn't your typical gateway community, given that it's located some 50 miles upstream from the Stillwater and Fallon National Wildlife Refuges. But water use in Reno has a dramatic effect on the two refuges, since they all share water from the Truckee River. Unfortunately, the majority of homes in Reno pay a flat fee for water use, giving residents little incentive to conserve water. In 1994, however, Reno began installing water meters at each local residence, charging customers for the amount of water they use. "If we don't have meters, we're not using water efficiently," says Janet Carson of Sierra Pacific Power, the local utility. The meters, which are financed by an impact fee assessed on new development in the city, will be installed in every home by the year 2005. Without such measures, the refuges would be unable to maintain wetlands that provide important staging and breeding areas for migratory birds.

• The Kenai River is the most popular recreational river in Alaska and one of the best salmon runs in the Pacific Northwest. The river's salmon fishery—both commercial and sport—contributes more than $41 million a year to the local economy. One reason is that the upper watershed of the river is protected by the Kenai National Wildlife Refuge, a 1.9-million-acre network of streams and lakes feeding into the river. But according to the

*Fishermen crowd a hot-spot on Alaska's Kenai River in a ritual known locally as "combat fishing." To safeguard the river and its fishery, the Borough of Kenai Peninsula provides tax credits to landowners who undertake bank restoration projects. (Alaska State Parks, courtesy of The Nature Conservancy)*

Alaska Department of Fish and Game, fish habitat in the lower reaches of the river is threatened by heavy foot traffic and construction of docks and landings along the riverbanks. To safeguard the fishery, the Borough of Kenai Peninsula provides landowners who undertake bank restoration projects with a three-year tax credit of up to 50 percent of their property taxes or 50 percent of the cost of the project, whichever is less. Eligible projects include cabling bundles of trees to the bank and replacing footpaths along the bank with steps or boardwalks. The tax credit applies only to the land portion of a property, not to homes and buildings; on an average parcel with 100 feet of river frontage, participating landowners would get a $250 annual credit for three years. The restoration projects don't benefit just fish. "You're going to have your land a lot longer" if you protect your river frontage, says Lisa Parker, Kenai Borough's planner. With nearly half the land along the Kenai River in private hands, more than 1,300 landowners qualify. The borough combines its tax incentive with an ordinance that restricts development in a 50-foot corridor along both sides of the river.

• When Lowell, Massachusetts, restricted the demolition of historic buildings and developed guidelines for their renovation, city leaders also persuaded local bankers to provide low-interest loans for rehabilitating buildings. Thirteen local banks each allocated 0.05 percent of their assets to a low-interest loan pool earmarked for restoration of buildings in the town's historic district. More than $300,000 was made available in 1975. Four years later, buoyed by the program's success, local bankers contributed another $300,000 to the loan pool.

• Vermont combines a statewide land-use planning statute, Act 250, with an innovative program to provide affordable housing for residents and protect farms and natural lands from development. In the 1980s alone, Vermont lost 10 percent of its dairy farms and saw housing prices increase by nearly 50 percent. With these trends showing no signs of leveling off, the state in 1987 established the Vermont Housing and Conservation Board, which has built more than 3,500 units of affordable housing, purchased 35,000 acres of land for conservation and recreation, and acquired development rights on 122 farms totaling more than 41,000 acres. The board often melds its priorities: In several transactions, it has purchased development rights on most of a farm, then recouped its costs by developing and selling affordable housing on acreage not subject to the agricultural preservation easement. Funding is derived primarily from the Vermont State Legislature, which has allocated $75 million to the board since 1987. The board leverages these dollars with money from federal agencies, nonprofit organizations, businesses, individuals, and local governments.

• Citizens in Red Lodge, Montana, a community of 2,000 people on the eastern edge of Yellowstone National Park, want new homes and buildings in their town to honor their western traditions. But they also want to minimize intrusion on the private-property rights that many westerners hold sacred. The community felt that in many cases unsightly architecture could be prevented merely by informing new property owners of local attitudes and preferences. Red Lodge residents have produced a short video on the town's history and sense of community, which is required viewing for anyone applying for a building permit.

• Kent County, Maryland, a gateway to the Chesapeake Bay, restricts development of its farmland and also gives farmers an incentive to keep their lands in production. A scattered large-lot subdivision in any of the county's designated "agricultural zones" is limited to one home per 30 acres. But by clustering that housing on a few acres and protecting the rest of the property as farmland or open space, the developer can triple density to one home per 10 acres.

Many gateway communities have found that local land acquisition programs are necessary to meet community priorities. Here are a few examples
of market-driven programs to buy important land and open space:

• In Monroe County, Florida, the gateway to four national wildlife refuges
in the Florida Keys, voters in 1988 approved a "tourist impact tax" that fi-
nances land acquisition through a 1 percent tax on hotel and motel rooms.
Half the revenue goes to the county general fund as compensation for the
loss of property-tax revenue resulting from publicly owned land. The other
half supports the Monroe County Land Authority, a local agency that has
bought more than 1,000 acres of wetlands, wildlife habitat, and recreation
sites, as well as real estate that is made available to affordable housing groups
like Habitat for Humanity. The Authority also buys properties whose land
value has been lowered by local environmental regulations. "Many of our
purchases compensate landowners for property the county doesn't want to
see developed because of its high environmental value," says director Mark
Rosch. In 1994, the Authority received $1.1 million from the tax and another
$400,000 from a 50-cent surcharge on admissions to three state parks in the
Keys. "The natural resources of the Keys are a lot of the reason that people
come here," Rosch says. "We need to protect them if we're going to sustain
our economy."

• Little Compton, an oceanfront community on the Rhode Island Sound,
protects its agricultural economy by buying conservation easements from
farmers. The program, which voters approved by a three-to-one margin, is
funded with a 2 percent transfer tax on local real estate transactions. Every
time a property changes hands, the buyer pays the town a fee equal to 2 percent of the purchase price. More than $150,000 a year is raised. Since
1986, the trust has made 30 acquisitions, totaling 650 acres.

• For 20 years, residents of Washington State's Methow Valley—the eastern entry to North Cascades National Park—fought a downhill-ski resort
proposed in their community. When the R.D. Merrill Company acquired
the property in 1993, its executives quickly recognized that any development plans needed local support. The company immediately began working
with community members to find a mutually acceptable use of the land.
After discussions, local residents agreed to support a smaller-scale, cross-
country-ski resort on the condition that Merrill impose a 1 percent sur-
charge on all property transactions within the resort. This market-derived
source of revenue will be used to purchase conservation easements—from
willing sellers only—on other private lands in the valley. Merrill also offered

to help finance a new organization, the Methow Valley Conservancy, which will restore fish and wildlife habitat in the valley and offer environmental education programs to residents and visitors.

• In Sonoma County, California, voters in 1990 approved a 0.25 percent county sales tax to finance the purchase of open space and development rights on farmland. The tax raises more than $10 million a year, most of which is used to purchase conservation easements from willing sellers. So far, more than 7,000 acres have been protected, including vineyards and ranches, community entrance ways, and the open spaces and scenic views so important to Sonoma County's tourism industry and quality of life.

• Since 1980, Vail, Colorado, gateway to the White River National Forest and a popular ski resort, has purchased open space, athletic fields, and trail corridors with the proceeds from a transfer tax on real estate sales within town limits. Vail adopted the program after citizens identified open-space protection as one of the community's top priorities. Approved by referendum, the tax now generates $2 million a year for open-space acquisi-

*Crested Butte, Colorado, taps the proceeds from a 2.25 percent real estate transfer tax to finance the acquisition of open space and conservation easements on lands important to the community. Many gateway communities have found that local land acquisition programs are necessary to meet community priorities. (Town of Crested Butte)*

tion; today, Vail owns and manages nearly 1,000 acres of parks and natural areas. In 1979, voters in nearby Crested Butte approved a 0.75 percent real estate transfer tax to purchase open space and conservation easements. Twelve years later, a developer's acquisition of a key parcel in a mountain pass above the town prompted voters to increase the tax to 2.25 percent so the open-space program can compete with private developers.

• Municipal bonds also can raise money to purchase land. In Missoula, Montana, a gateway to the Lolo National Forest, voters in 1995 approved a $5 million bond issue to buy public open space, trails, river corridors, and parks in several predesignated areas. The first revenue will purchase a 1,300-acre parcel near the summit of Mount Jumbo, which overlooks the city and is an important elk wintering area. Before the bond act passed, the city went through a comprehensive planning process that laid out an open-space system and identified the lands to be protected. As a result, the bond act passed by more than a two-to-one margin. "People saw where their money would be going," says Kate Supplee, Missoula's open-space planner. Although the bond issue will increase property taxes on an average Missoula home by about $27 a year, it will help the city deal with a growth spurt that has threatened to alter its small-town character. "Having money to purchase open space allows us to accommodate growth but preserve what leads to that growth in the first place," says Greg Tollefson, one of the organizers.

• In 1967, and again in 1989, citizens in Boulder, Colorado approved a citywide sales tax to support the protection of open space, mountain views, greenways, and farm and ranchland around the city (see case study in chapter 2 for more details). Seven-tenths of a cent of every dollar spent in Boulder supports the city's acquisition of land and conservation easements. All told, more than 25,000 acres in and around Boulder have been protected from development.

Voluntary contributions or donations from local citizens also can supplement government programs. The challenge is to create an atmosphere that encourages philanthropy and civic pride:

• Drinking water on Cape Cod, Massachusetts, is derived entirely from underground aquifers. Although local land-use statutes discourage development of the wetlands that recharge aquifers, an association of land trusts on the Cape found that appealing to the philanthropic spirit of local people also could help protect drinking water. With information obtained from tax records, the association mailed each wetland owner—nearly 5,000 people—a brochure on the importance of wetlands and the tax advantages of donating conservation easements on them. In several communities, public workshops were held to follow up on the brochures. So far, 17 landowners have donated easements on more than 100 acres of wetlands.

• In Aspen, Colorado, a local land trust has created a fund that landowners can tap for one free session with a tax attorney or financial advisor. In areas with pricey real estate, conservation easements can provide landowners with relief from high property and estate taxes. But because a short meeting with a tax attorney can cost as much as $150, "many landowners have an initial reluctance to meet with them," says Chuck Vidal, director of the Aspen Valley Land Trust. Once the many financial benefits of easements are made clear, however, landowners often continue the consultations and end up donating easements. Already, the fund has led to the protection of two important properties. Vidal says, "These came about simply from us being able to say, 'Why don't you go talk to an attorney? We'll help pay for it.'"

• In Ashland, Wisconsin, a gateway to Apostle Islands National Lakeshore, the Sigurd Olson Environmental Institute provides realtors with information packets that help new owners of waterfront property minimize their impacts on loons, a migratory water bird highly sensitive to human activity. Realtors distribute the packets to clients who buy waterfront homes. The institute has also recruited more than 750 citizens to conduct loon surveys, monitor water quality, and teach children and adults about loons. Apostle Islands is made up of 21 islands in Lake Superior, which, along with the hundreds of smaller lakes in northern Wisconsin, provide important breeding areas for the loon.

• The Foothills Land Conservancy, a nonprofit group in Maryville, Tennessee, exemplifies how fund-raising campaigns can motivate and involve a community. In August 1994, the conservancy bought a one-year option on a 4,600-acre property next to Great Smoky Mountains National Park and immediately initiated a campaign to raise the $1.3 million purchase price. The conservancy used radio, television, and newspaper coverage to appeal for donations. It also prepared a color brochure stressing the property's importance to wildlife, local scenery, and the economy. Ten months later, the conservancy was able to purchase the property with the help of contributions from more than 3,300 people, including 100 school and 4-H groups. One elementary school raised more than $2,000 at an after-school dance, raffle, and bake sale. "Not only did we purchase an important property," says conservancy director Randy Brown, "we got a lot of people involved in protecting the foothills region."

## Conservation Easements

Conservation easements allow landowners to realize financial benefits from their land without selling or subdividing their property. Their flexibility and effectiveness make them applicable to a variety of land uses.

To understand how conservation easements work, it is first necessary to understand the nature of real estate. Legally, real estate can be thought of as a "bundle" of property rights, which includes the right to farm or ranch, to construct buildings, to subdivide the land, to restrict access, to harvest timber, or to mine. In many instances, a right can be separated from the bundle and transferred to another party. Mineral rights to property, for example, are commonly bought and sold separately from surface rights.

Conservation easements involve the purchase or donation of a property's development rights. An easement permanently extinguishes these rights so that a property can never be developed. The land remains on the tax rolls, in private ownership, and can be sold to others or passed on to heirs.

Easements are tailored to each particular property and to the needs of each individual landowner. Agricultural preservation easements, for example, allow continued farming or ranching and do not include public access. Easements can be placed on an entire tract of land or on only part of a property. In many cases, conservation easements allow "limited development" or commercial use of part of the land, so long as these activities do not affect the land's conservation value.

Easement restrictions are typically permanent and "run with the land," binding the original landowner and all future landowners. Like all property rights, conservation easements are recorded with the county clerk so that future owners and lenders will know about restrictions when they obtain title reports.

Easements can offer significant tax benefits to landowners. Landowners who donate easements or sell them below market value can receive income tax deductions for the value of their charitable donation. Landowners also can benefit from lower estate and property taxes since their property is stripped of its development rights.

Case Study

# Calvert County, Maryland

*Regulations clearly are important to help safeguard quality of life. But all too often communities fail to couple them with nonregulatory measures like tax incentives, public education, and voluntary programs that encourage residents to get involved. On the shores of Chesapeake Bay, Calvert County found that preserving its rural flavor required an innovative "transfer of development rights" program that channels growth to appropriate areas without penalizing land-*

*owners outside designated growth boundaries. By offering low-interest loans to land-conservation organizations, the county also encourages citizens' groups to play a part in protecting farmland and securing open space.*

Calvert County is bounded on three sides by water. To the east is the nation's largest estuary, the Chesapeake Bay; to the west and south is the Patuxent River, Maryland's second-longest river.

Like other rural counties on the fringes of major metropolitan areas (both Baltimore and Washington are within commuting distance), Calvert County is buckling under rapid growth. The county's population grew from 35,000 in 1980 to more than 51,000 in 1990, nearly a 50 percent increase. County officials recognized that they needed a growth management strategy, but they wanted to make sure that local people supported it. The county held a series of public meetings designed to inform residents of growth trends and management tools. Afterwards, officials solicited ideas for maintaining the area's quality of life.

"Before we undertook any initiative, we got the people here invested in the process," says Greg Bowen, deputy director of the county's planning and zoning department. "Citizens have to be involved every step of the way, from the identification of problems to the selection of solutions."

With strong public support, the county settled on two innovative and market-oriented initiatives to influence the development process: a transfer of development rights (TDR) program that counters urban sprawl and a revolving loan fund to support land conservation. Both programs make use of market forces as a way of meeting the county's goals.

The TDR program creates a framework under which landowners can transfer development rights from protection zones, or "sending areas," to growth centers, or "receiving areas." Sending areas are lands that warrant protection, which can include anything from farmlands to wetlands. By contrast, receiving areas are towns and other urban areas where future growth is desired. Once the county designated its sending and receiving areas, the marketplace took over.

Here's an example of how the program works: Say a landowner has a 10-acre lot in one of the county's predesignated receiving areas. Under county zoning laws, the property could be developed at 2 homes per acre—20 houses in all. Using the TDR program, however, the landowner can increase the development density of the property by acquiring development rights from a farmer in the sending area and then transferring these rights to the 10-acre lot in the receiving area. For example, since the zoning density in the sending area is one house per five acres, the urban landowner could double his or her housing density by purchasing the development rights on

*Agricultural and open land in Calvert County, Maryland, like this farm, is quickly being converted to housing for commuters to Washington, D.C., and Annapolis. To stem the loss of farmland and protect its rural flavor, the county has combined a transfer of development rights program with a low-interest loan program that helps fund acquisition of sensitive lands. (Ed McMahon)*

100 acres in the sending area and transferring them to the urban property.
Once the development rights are purchased on those acres, that property is
forever dedicated to agricultural use or open space.

Calvert County has designated 17,000 acres of farmland and forest land
as sending areas from which development rights can be transferred. So far,
landowners in these areas have sold development rights on more than 4,000
acres. Five receiving areas also have been established, each located within
or near town centers. The county's zoning ordinance in sending areas is one
home per five acres, so a developer needs to buy five acres of development
rights in a sending area—which cost about $11,500—to acquire the right to
erect one additional house in a receiving area. In 1995, roughly 100 development rights were traded.

The TDR program is popular with farmers and other rural landowners because it controls sprawl without penalizing them for owning property outside designated growth areas. Developers also like TDR because it specifies
where growth can occur and also gives them a means for increasing density.

Nonetheless, Bowen cautions that TDR will work only when there's a
market for development rights. "There's got to be enough TDRs sold so that
a farmer or landowner has reasonable assurance that his development rights
will be purchased," he says.

Calvert County couples its TDR program with a $1 million revolving loan
fund from which local nonprofit organizations can borrow to purchase open
space within the county. Borrowers can repay the loans in part by enrolling
the purchased land in Calvert County's TDR program and selling the development rights.

One advantage of the loan program is that it allows Calvert County to
achieve its land-conservation objectives without assuming the fiscal burden
of managing land. Dollars from the fund, which was created in 1994 with
county tax revenue, are limited to those projects that an advisory committee
already has identified as priorities. These include farmland, environmentally
sensitive areas, historic sites, new playing fields and town parks, or buffers
around existing parks. All loans require borrowers to place permanent conservation easements on the land.

So far, funds have been used for two acquisitions: The Plum Point Land
Trust secured a $600,000 loan to acquire a farm on Chesapeake Bay, while
the American Chestnut Land Trust borrowed $200,000 to purchase a prop-
erty in a pristine watershed.

Although borrowers are not charged interest, they are assessed a 1 percent fee to defray the administrative costs of the program. Borrowers have
five years to repay half the loan and ten years to repay all of it. As the re-
payments trickle in, the county can begin financing other projects. "By the

fifth year of the program," says Sherrod Sturrock, capital projects coordinator for the county, "we'll have enough funds to make another loan."

## Meet the Needs of Both Landowner and Community

In most communities, problems don't result from development itself, but from the patterns of development: where it takes place, how it's laid out, and what it looks like.

Communities need to maintain a balance between various land uses—commercial and residential, large lot and small lot, farmland and industrial. This requires that they not simply export problematic land uses, but that they work closely with landowners and developers upfront to make sure that development is done responsibly and to see that it meets local needs and priorities. It also requires that they court reputable developers who are willing to do more than what's mandated by law and who work closely with the entire community, not just a few officials, throughout the development process.

In most communities, problems aren't usually caused by development itself, but by the patterns of development: where it takes place, how it's laid out, and what it looks like. (The Conservation Foundation)

Successful gateway communities also scrutinize development proposals against a range of criteria: Does the development cover the cost of the public services needed by the people who will live there? Is it in line with the community's vision for its future? How will it affect local resources and quality of life?

Conversely, communities that expect landowners and developers to produce a responsible product must also recognize that developers have legitimate expectations as well. Developers who are willing to incorporate the public interest into their projects have a right to expect flexible communities willing to modify standard zoning and engineering requirements. A community visioning process can assist developers by giving them advance notice of the kind of development preferred by the community. "It helps to know what the rules are up front, before investments are made," says Peter Backus, a landowner and developer in Arizona.

Successful gateway communities also have the ability to recognize, and the courage to reject, development that doesn't enhance local values. At the same time, they should realize that they can't deal with the challenge of growth simply by resisting all change.

Here are a few examples of communities that have harnessed the development process to their benefit:

• In Washington County, Utah, gateway to Zion National Park, developers and conservationists are working together to preserve open space and quality of life. In 1995, five of the county's leading developers agreed to donate between $100 and $500 to the Virgin River Land Preservation Association for every home or lot they sell. The association will use the proceeds, which could total $600,000 over the next decade, to purchase scenic backdrops, conservation easements on farmland, and public recreation sites, including access to the Virgin River. "Everyone wins," says developer Rick Sant. "We preserve open space, but fairly compensate the owner of the property." Over the next 20 years, Sant's firm alone will donate funds from the sale of 1,200 lots.

• In 1986, Ventura County, California, received two separate proposals for large-scale residential and resort developments. Both properties bordered the Santa Monica Mountains National Recreation Area, a patchwork of federal, state, and private lands on the outskirts of Los Angeles and one of the largest undeveloped stretches of land in Southern California. Wanting to safeguard the integrity of its few public lands, the Ventura County Board of Supervisors merged the two proposals into a single development clustered on one of the properties. The county then conditioned approval of the project on the property owner—the Ahmanson Land Company—setting aside open space, providing affordable housing, and constructing a network of public trails that connects with existing trails in the park. Under the arrangement, the Park Service will pay the other property owner, comedian Bob Hope, fair market value for his land. "This solution met the needs of the two landowners, future homeowners in the project, and the entire community," says Supervisor Maria VanderKolk. Ventura County's proactive stance isn't limited to this project: The county withholds development approval for up to one year on any parcel the Park Service has expressed interest in, giving the agency time to purchase the property if the landowner is willing to sell.

• After years of battling protests from residents, Wal-Mart finally opened its first discount superstore in Vermont. In September 1995, Wal-Mart store No. 2,158 opened in Bennington, but only after substantial concessions to the community. The Bennington store is half the size of a normal Wal-Mart and occupies an old Woolworth department store rather than a new site on the outskirts of town. "They took an existing retail facility and made it into a Wal-Mart," says Steve Juszczyk, Bennington's zoning administrator. "They didn't take a virgin piece of farmland and turn it into a new store." In two other Vermont communities, St. Albans and St. Johnsbury, citizens groups are fighting proposed Wal-Marts. The reason: fears that the discounter would bankrupt locally owned businesses and turn downtowns into ghost towns. In St. Albans, a state panel estimated that it would cost the community $2.67 for every dollar of benefit generated by a Wal-Mart.

• In 1975, Cannon Beach, Oregon, gateway to several state parks on Oregon's Pacific Coast, enacted a zoning ordinance that prohibits "formula food restaurants," defined as any restaurant with a standardized menu and exterior design. The town designed the ordinance to preserve its distinctive character and protect locally owned restaurants and shops.

• Before 1995, Marine on St. Croix, Minnesota, a community on the banks of the St. Croix River, a nationally designated wild and scenic river, had tried to protect open space by limiting residential subdivisions in rural areas to one home for every five acres. But when a developer proposed to subdivide 175 acres on the outskirts of town, citizens realized they wanted more than a large-lot subdivision. "That was one of the few open properties left here," says zoning administrator Ginger Bolin, "and the community wanted to make sure it was done right." The city put a temporary moratorium on building permits then drew up a new "cluster" ordinance that retains the one-home-per-five-acres density, but also requires the developer to protect half the parcel as open space. Ownership of the open space must be transferred to either the city, a local homeowners' association, or an established land trust. A judge upheld the law when a local developer and two property owners tried to block its implementation.

• Martin County, Florida, is the site of Hobe Sound National Wildlife Refuge, a 970-acre refuge that protects sea turtle nesting areas on the Atlantic Coast. The refuge includes 3.5 miles of undeveloped beaches, a vanishing commodity on the Florida coast. Using impact fees, which have become an increasingly popular way to assure that development pays for its demands on local resources and facilities, the county has developed its own beach protection program. Each new development in Martin County is assessed a one-time fee dedicated to purchasing beachfront property. For each project, the county estimates the number of new residents, the average amount of beach needed per person, and the market price for a linear foot of beach. In 1995, each new single-family home paid a beach fee of $169. Martin County also uses impact fees to finance boat ramps, libraries, and local park acquisition and maintenance.

• Like many counties surrounding Yellowstone National Park, Park County, Wyoming, is experiencing a housing boom that has driven up real estate prices to the point that many residents can no longer find affordable homes. To preserve the county's character, the board of commissioners in 1993 decided to defer all zoning changes until the county had time to complete a new land-use plan. The moratorium was imposed after a landowner informed the county of plans to develop a strip of retail outlets on the eastern entrance road to Yellowstone. "We were about to see neons and 7-11s on a wonderful stretch of highway," says Colin Simpson, an attorney in Cody, the county seat and the self-proclaimed rodeo capital of the world. "A moratorium isn't a solution in and of itself," says Mike Patrick, a furniture maker and member of the Park County zoning board, "but it gave us the time to do a plan right."

### Case Study

## The True Costs of Development

From a fiscal standpoint, it's almost always better for a gateway community to plan for ordered use of the land around a park or refuge than it is to allow helter-skelter development that requires heavy government investment in infrastructure and public services.

Most local governments are happy to see new housing subdivisions rise on their outskirts. Doesn't such development expand the tax base? Yes, but each new house also means another trash can to empty, more children to enroll in and bus to school, another stretch of road to maintain, a new sewer line, another residence to protect from theft and fire, and so on.

Many communities are discovering that the tax revenue from sprawling, low-density residential development rarely offsets the cost of providing these services. In fact, residential development of farms, ranches, and raw land outside a town's core nearly always results in a revenue shortfall. The reason is that while rural and open lands may produce fewer tax dollars than developed areas, they also cost less to service.

A recent study by the U.S. Department of Agriculture and the American Farmland Trust concluded that for every dollar of tax revenue collected from residential land uses, local governments spend an average of $1.36 to provide services. By contrast, for every dollar received from agricultural land uses, local governments spend only 21 cents. Much of the difference is attributable to school costs. "Cows don't go to school," the study noted wryly.

Many communities are beginning to take notice:

• Huntsville, Alabama, is the eastern gateway to Wheeler National Wildlife Refuge, a 35,000-acre preserve along the Tennessee River. Huntsville's eastern limits are flanked by Monte Sano Mountain, the city's most visible landmark. In 1988, a developer acquired a large tract on the western slope of the mountain and proposed to convert it to high priced homes. An analysis by a local conservation organization, the Huntsville Land Trust, determined that it would cost the city about $5 million to install roads, sewers, and other infrastructure for the development, and another $1.4 million a year to service it. On the other hand, the city could acquire the entire parcel for $3 million, with annual maintenance costs of only about $40,000. Once voters discovered the true cost of the development, they approved a sales-tax increase to buy the property and dedicate it as a park.

• Visitors to Lake Michigan's eastern shore often combine a trip to Sleeping Bear Dunes National Lakeshore with a visit to nearby Old Mission Peninsula, where cherry orchards and vineyards dot a narrow finger of land that juts 16 miles into Grand Traverse Bay. Concerned with their town's rapid growth, voters in 1994 approved a property-tax increase to purchase conservation easements on farms, preventing them from ever being developed. Support for the tax hike was based on estimates that a surging population would lead to higher municipal expenses and, eventually, higher taxes. In other words, a slight increase in property taxes today could avert a larger

*These cherry orchards on Michigan's Old Mission Peninsula represent a signifi-cant part of the local economy. Concerned with rapid growth, local residents voted to purchase conservation easements on the peninsula's farms, thereby compensat-ing farmers who want to keep their land in agriculture. More and more communi-ties are discovering that the tax revenue from sprawling, low-density residential development rarely offsets the cost of providing services to new homeowners. (Grand Traverse Conservancy)*

increase tomorrow. Over the next 15 years, the tax increase will raise $2.6 million, enough to buy development rights on nearly one-fourth of the peninsula's farms.

• Yarmouth, Maine, a community on the state's rugged Atlantic Coast, chartered a citizens committee to examine the pros and cons of developing a parcel of land outside the town. The committee found that (1) if the prop-erty were developed, service costs would be $140,000 a year greater than the tax revenue the project would generate, and (2) the city could purchase the entire property for $76,000 a year over a 20-year period. As a result, resi-dents overwhelmingly approved a referendum to issue $1.5 million in bonds for open-space acquisition.

Other communities have learned the hard way:

• Carbon County, Montana, is a gateway to both Yellowstone National Park and the Absaroka–Beartooth Wilderness Area in the Custer National

Forest. In the mid-1980s, county officials agreed to finance the infrastructure for a private golf course and residential development slated for a ranch outside the town of Red Lodge. Unfortunately, the county based its decision on the developer's overly optimistic financial projections. When the project went bankrupt a few years later, Carbon County had to allocate 10 percent of its 1989 and 1990 budgets to a court-ordered debt payment plan. "We ponied up $150,000 a year for two years and are still paying about $6,000 a year," says Carbon County attorney Tony Kendall.

• Loudoun County, Virginia, is famous for its horse farms and country estates. It's also at the edge of the Washington, D.C., metropolitan area, one of the nation's fastest-growing regions, where subdivisions are rapidly replacing prime pasture and farmland. Researchers have found that while the county receives annual tax revenues of between $2.7 million and $2.9 million for every 1,000 dwellings, the cost to service them averages between $3.5 million and $5.0 million a year.

• Although a surge in tourism has stimulated a boom in the construction and real estate industries on Mount Desert Island, Maine, gateway to Acadia National Park, it hasn't come without a cost. According to the local League of Women Voters, from 1977 to 1986 the town of Mount Desert's fire-fighting budget skyrocketed from $13,211 to $85,283, its police budget from $49,235 to $195,840, and its streets and roads budget from $219,441 to $492,016.

Case Study
===
## Tucson, Arizona

*Sunny Tucson is one of the top winter destinations in the United States. But many residents fear that a flurry of resort development threatens the city's desert ecosystems and Southwestern charm. Faced with a proposal for a large resort adjacent to Saguaro National Park, Tucson leaders asked environmentalists, national park officials, and the developer to iron out their differences and create an environmentally friendly project. The result is a scaled-back resort that protects sensitive areas, provides a return for the developer, and, through a system of fees and deed restrictions, raises money to protect the Sonoran Desert.*

Saguaro National Park's two units sit like bookends on the east and west sides of metropolitan Tucson, protecting nearly 92,000 acres of Sonoran

Desert. The park takes its name from the tall green saguaro cactus which thrives here and has become a symbol of the American Southwest.

When the park's eastern unit was created in 1933, the edges of the Tucson metro area were a distant 12 miles away. Tucson's growth over the past two decades, however, has pushed development to the park's very boundaries. In the mid-1980s, Superintendent Bill Paleck recognized that given sharp reductions in congressional funding for land acquisition, protecting the park's desert ecosystems would require cooperative efforts with adjacent landowners. Of particular concern was a 6,000-acre parcel, the Rocking K Ranch, which shared a five-mile boundary with the park's eastern unit. In 1989, the landowner had asked the county to approve a large-scale resort and residential development on the site.

Paleck knew that the county's existing land-use ordinances provided little protection for the park's wildlife; he also knew that the county board of supervisors would probably approve the project with few restrictions. So he decided to work with the Rocking K's owner to find a mutually acceptable plan for the ranch. A planned development that incorporated environmen-

*Faced with a proposal for a large resort adjacent to Tucson's Saguaro National Park, community leaders asked environmentalists, park officials, and the developer to iron out their differences and create an environmentally friendly project. The result is a scaled-back resort that protects sensitive areas, provides a return for the developer, and raises money to protect the Sonoran Desert through an innovative system of fees and deed restrictions. (National Park Service)*

tal safeguards, he reasoned, was preferable to the helter-skelter subdivision already occurring near other parts of the park.

The owner of the property also stood to gain from Park Service support for the project. "Quite honestly, we believe that environmentally sensitive development improves our bottom line, even if it means lower densities," says Chris Monson, the project's developer.

Paleck persuaded the Rocking K Development Company to invite local and national conservation groups, including the World Wildlife Fund and National Parks & Conservation Association, to critique the development plan for the ranch. The partnership eventually settled on three conditions it believed were necessary to protect the park:

1. The National Park Service would acquire 1,900 acres of sensitive wild-life habitat on the Rocking K and another 2,100 acres on an adjoining ranch.

2. More than half the total land area involved in the development, espe-cially riparian areas and steep slopes, would be permanently set aside as wildlife habitat, open space, or greenways.

3. A 2.5-mile stretch of overgrazed and dewatered stream on the property would be restored to its natural condition and devoted to wildlife and recreation.

With agreement on these conditions, the partnership next addressed the more difficult problem of how to assure that its conservation measures were carried out after the development had been completed. It proposed creating an independent, nonprofit organization—the Rincon Institute—to instill an environmental ethic into all aspects of the new community and to make sure that future builders and landowners honor the developer's environmental commitments.

Founded in 1990, the Rincon Institute conducts a range of conservation activities to protect the park and to increase public understanding of how development affects desert ecosystems. The Institute monitors wildlife pop-ulations, conducts environmental education programs, and manages natural lands on the site.

This innovative blend of conservation and development has attracted sup-port from a range of foundations, individuals, and state and federal conser-vation agencies. "The Rincon Institute is unique in its ability to craft win-win solutions that enhance park resources and enrich local economic opportunities," says Wilke Nelson of the National Park Foundation, one of the foundations that supports the Institute.

But what's most noteworthy about the Rincon Institute may be its future funding sources. Long-term funding for the institute's activities will come from surcharges on hotel rooms at the resort, occupancy fees levied on commercial and retail outlets on the site, and transfer taxes and monthly fees assessed to homeowners. Eventually, the development will generate between $200,000 and $300,000 a year for resource conservation adjacent to Saguaro National Park.

Organizations like the Rincon Institute won't resolve all the concerns about development along park and refuge boundaries. But where development adjacent to public lands is inevitable, or even desirable, the Rincon Institute model can substantially lessen the impacts on park or refuge resources. And perhaps just as important, it can ensure that the people who benefit from development pay for conservation.

## Team Up with Public Land Managers

Historically, the residents of gateway communities and managers of neighboring national parks, wildlife refuges, or other public lands have tended to view each other as adversaries rather than allies. In a growing number of places, however, public-land managers and gateway communities are creating mutually beneficial, or win-win, partnerships. To be sure, local residents and managers of public lands often have honest differences over a community's future direction. But their overall goals are increasingly similar: Both often agree on the need for open space, good jobs, clean air and water, productive land, and healthy, vital communities.

These shared goals give gateway communities and managers of public lands a starting point for working together. Across the country, many have teamed up on efforts to round out seasonal fluctuations in tourism, develop transportation systems that ease traffic congestion, or see that development and tourism don't detract from local values.

Perhaps the most important contribution a national park or wildlife refuge can make is to strengthen the local economy. Many partnerships between public lands and community leaders encourage visitors to frequent businesses in the town. Other partnerships have sought to ensure that the park or refuge purchases supplies from local businesses and hires local residents wherever possible. And as noted in chapter 2, other gateway communities have sought to benefit from the contribution that public lands make to local quality of life.

Managers of public lands also can offer something that's essential to any community embarking on a locally based initiative: financial and technical assistance. In fact, in many cases the legislation creating a national park or wildlife refuge encourages the land management agency to provide such assistance.

One stumbling block to productive relationships between gateway communities and the public lands on their borders is the rapid turnover of staff at many government agencies. Career ladders at land management agencies encourage managers to move from unit to unit and region to region to gain experience in a variety of settings. This means that a superintendent or refuge manager who establishes a constructive relationship with a community often moves on to a new assignment. "There needs to be people who work with communities on a regular basis," says Larry Gamble, a land-use specialist at Rocky Mountain National Park. "It takes a long time to build trusting relationships."

Gamble speaks from experience. Rocky Mountain National Park enjoys a productive relationship with the neighboring town of Estes Park largely because of Gamble, who is one of the few federal land management agency employees hired to work specifically on improving relationships with communities.

Here are a few other examples of gateway communities that have benefitted from working in partnership with nearby parks, refuges, or other public lands:

• At Glacier National Park, Montana, Superintendent Gil Lusk promoted good relations with nearby communities by forgoing the park superintendent's isolated house inside the park and instead living in the town of Kalispell. Delegating day-to-day operations of the park to an assistant, Lusk used his presence in the community to establish a dialogue with local residents and encourage them to reduce their impacts on the land surrounding the park. In exchange, Lusk pledged to oppose expansion of the park and to locate campgrounds and worker housing on private lands outside park boundaries. "As a manager of a public land, your job isn't just protecting the resource," he says. "It's protecting it in a way the community can support."

• In California's San Joaquin Valley, landowners with property adjacent to the San Luis National Wildlife Refuge have sold the refuge conservation easements on nearly 52,000 acres of privately owned wetlands. The easements allow neighboring landowners to continue farming, grazing, hunting, and fishing; at the same time, the refuge gains the assurance that the properties will never be converted to residential development. Meanwhile, refuge biologists and local landowners are jointly restoring the wetlands for the benefit of waterfowl and endangered species like the San Joaquin kit fox and blunt-nosed leopard lizard.

• At Mammoth Cave National Park, Kentucky, the Park Service helped local farmers obtain U.S. Department of Agriculture cost-share grants to install more than 80 animal waste-treatment units. Cleaner surface water and groundwater enhance the local environment and help protect the underground resources of the park.

• Eleven communities that border Cuyahoga Valley National Recreation Area, Ohio, have formed a council to coordinate land-use planning and establish guidelines for development along the park boundary. So far, guidelines have been approved for building height, density, and signs. Recommendations of the Cuyahoga Valley Communities Council are not binding, but landowners and developers usually implement them. For example, the council persuaded the owners of a new office building and warehouse facility on the western edge of the park to use landscaping and grading to shield the building and parking lot from the park. And, according to Cuyahoga superintendent John Debo, when the council drew up recommendations to protect park entry points, many of the gateway communities revised their zoning standards.

• The U.S. Department of the Interior's American Battlefield Protection Program provides communities adjacent to Civil War battlefields with technical assistance on land-use planning and design standards, financial assistance for land acquisition or planning, or help with inventorying and inter-

*In Ohio, the 11 communities surrounding Cuyahoga Valley National Recreation Area established a council to ensure that development doesn't clash with the scenic quality of the park. Throughout the country, communities and public land managers are teaming up on issues of mutual benefit. (Robert Glenn Ketchum)*

preting battlefields. Each year, more than $400,000 in grants is allocated. Funds have been used in Resaca, Georgia, to inform landowners of the benefits of conservation easements; in Corinth, Mississippi, to prepare museum exhibits; in Pilot Knob, Missouri, to conduct archeological surveys; and in Gettysburg, Pennsylvania, to develop a historical downtown walking tour.

• In Fort Scott, Kansas, home of the Fort Scott National Historic Site, a U.S. Army outpost built in 1842, city leaders sought the Park Service's assistance in remaking its downtown in a frontier-era motif. First, the city designated its downtown as a historic district where exterior remodeling must receive approval from a municipal panel. Then, to encourage private action, the city redesigned its sidewalks, trash receptacles, and street lights. Park officials help by providing the 80,000 annual visitors to the historic site with brochures about local businesses and points of interest. The cooperative approach taken by the city and park has resulted in a longer tourist season and in the start-up of new businesses such as bed and breakfasts and antique shops. "You wouldn't have these types of businesses without all the work the community has done," says Steve Miller, superintendent of the park.

• In the 1960s and 1970s, Cape Cod National Seashore, Massachusetts, was created with the acquisition of 45,000 acres of beaches, dunes, and barrier islands on the Atlantic Coast. When federal acquisition efforts slowed in the 1980s, local governments picked up the slack. Voters in five of the six communities that adjoin the national seashore—Chatham, Eastham, Orleans, Truro, and Wellfleet—have approved local acquisitions of open space Between 1985 and 1988, these towns purchased more than $18 million of wildlife habitat, aquifer recharge areas, and other conservation properties. Each purchase was approved by a two-thirds vote at a town meeting then put to voters in bond acts requiring townwide approval.

• City of Rocks National Reserve, Idaho, preserves a section of the California Trail that weaves its way through a number of towering granite monoliths. The rocks furnished westward travelers with an easily recognized landmark and resting place. To encourage local participation in the reserve's first management plan, park officials asked the Cassia County Board of Commissioners to appoint several citizens to help decide what, if any, facilities should be erected in the park. In the meantime, City of Rocks helped the county obtain federal funding to designate a local road as a scenic byway. "Both the park and the county want City of Rocks to be the keystone of a bigger package," says David Pugh, the park superintendent.

• Salem, Massachusetts, is a historic, Colonial-era town best known for its witch trials of the 17th century. In an effort to enhance Salem's tourist appeal, a diverse group of town officials, residents, and representatives from the Salem Maritime National Historic Site, Salem State College, and several local museums joined forces to create an extensive trail network through the town. The trails connect the downtown commercial area with tourist attractions, neighborhood parks, residential areas, and the national historic site, which celebrates Salem's years as America's busiest port. Before establishment of the trail system, the partnership took steps to resolve landowners' concerns. This cooperative approach led to several modifications—smaller signs, for example—that galvanized community support for the trail system. The partnership also is working to alleviate downtown parking problems, rehabilitate historic buildings, and promote public understanding of Salem's role in the nation's history.

• Two national parks—Zion in Utah and Rocky Mountain in Colorado—have proposed building new visitor centers on adjoining private lands. By locating the visitor centers outside their boundaries, the parks avoid direct impacts to parkland and also allow neighboring landowners both to contribute to, and benefit from, the environmental values of the park. In both instances, landowners are putting up the bulk of the construction and maintenance costs.

---

### Tips for Park and Refuge Managers

Here are some suggestions for park and refuge managers who want to build partnerships with the communities and landowners on their borders:

*Know Thy Neighbor.* Take the time to get to know local leaders. Working relationships with community members are best developed outside of hearing rooms or council chambers. Don't limit your activities to an occasional open house or reception for the community—have lunch regularly with community leaders; give them tours of the park or refuge; or arrange a hunting, hiking, or fishing trip. Be sure to interact not just with elected officials but with everyone involved in local decision making: bankers, developers, environmental advocates, landowners, journalists, land-use planners, and business owners. Make sure you're visible before controversy arises.

*Become a Member of the Community.* Developing good relationships requires a full-time commitment to the well-being of the community. Be willing to tackle more than just those issues of importance to your park or refuge; participate in the whole range of issues affecting the community. Get involved in the community as well—join a neighborhood association, coach a Little League team, volunteer on community projects, join the Rotary, or become an active member of a church. If possible, locate employee housing in the community rather than behind the park boundary.

*Get Involved Early and Often.* Effective participation in a community's decision-making process requires early and ongoing involvement. The best opportunity to influence decision making occurs well before proposals are made public. This principle works both ways: Don't expect to be invited to a community's preliminary planning sessions if you don't include local leaders in your own.

*Be a Team Player.* As a member of the community, you are entitled to participate in local decision-making processes and express concerns and opinions. Accept that you are only one of many who are trying to shape and influence decisions. Constructive participation in community decision making will only enhance your role as a legitimate member of the community.

*Build Coalitions.* Having a well-organized and thoughtful constituency is the best way to ensure that local government listens to park or refuge concerns. A coalition of individuals or groups working toward a common goal can be extremely effective in influencing decisions. Involving too many people is always better than leaving someone out. Establish partnerships between divergent interest groups—an alliance between a downtown merchants association and a local "Friends of the Refuge" group, for example, can have a powerful effect on local decisions. And do it before you need to—a proactive group is typically more effective than one that organizes in response to a specific threat or protest.

*Develop a Strategy.* Don't go blindly into partnerships or community relationships; Have a strategy and tangible goals in mind. Understand both the concerns most important to you and those where compromise can be sought. Instead of opposing projects, try to suggest modifications that would allow you to support them or alternatives that allow you to present your concerns in a positive light.

*Don't Get Ruffled by Criticism.* Some members of the community will not appreciate your views. Expect criticism and accept it without becoming defensive. Resist the temptation to fire back. It's important to maintain an open dialogue not only with those who share your views but with individuals and groups who may oppose you. Know which relationships will lead to fruitful partnerships and which will simply keep the lines of communication open.

*Understand the Full Range of Growth Management Strategies.* Many local officials are unaware or suspicious of growth management tools. To ease doubts about growth management, every manager of public lands should be familiar with the complete spectrum of public and private land-use techniques—conservation easements, agricultural districts, cluster development, floodplain regulations, zoning, etc.—and how they apply in your state or locality.

*Lead by Example.* Wherever possible, public-land managers should set the standard for new development. If a new park or refuge facility is under consideration, involve the community in determining its location and scale. Then design the facility as a model for other projects in the community. Utilize architecture that blends in with the landscape, outside lighting that keeps night skies dark, landscaping that makes use of native plants, and conservation-minded plumbing and lighting. (Older buildings can be retrofitted, too.) Use interpretive signs and brochures to make sure the public knows what's been done.

*Demonstrate the Link between Resource Protection and Economic Vitality.* Local leaders are more likely to pay attention to environmental concerns if they can be connected with economic vitality. Develop data that demonstrate how your unit of public land contributes to the local economy through increased property values, tourism, sales-tax revenue, local purchases, or jobs. A local college might be able to help carry out this research. Also, wherever possible, hire from the community and purchase products and services from local businesses.

*Thanks to Gil Lusk for help in assembling these suggestions.*

Case Study

# Moab, Utah

*Many gateway communities don't realize that the managers of public lands on their borders can be powerful allies. In Moab, residents found that a campaign to increase visitation resulted in a surge in tourism that tripled property values, required a hefty investment in law enforcement officers, and forced the county to procure an expensive new landfill for its mountains of trash. To control recreation use and restore damaged landscapes, Moab leaders have formed a new coalition that couples local energy and ideas with the many resources available through government land management agencies.*

Southern Utah is famous for its red-rock canyons, natural arches, and twisted rock formations that seem to change color with each movement of the sun. The region's beauty prompted Franklin Delano Roosevelt's Interior Secretary Harold Ickes to suggest that all of southern Utah be designated as one immense park.

Utah's rugged appearance, however, belies a fragility common to arid landscapes. The southern portion of the state receives an average of only seven inches of rainfall a year, making it slow to recover from human impacts. "Does it ever rain in this country, ranger?" author Edward Abbey recounts being asked when he worked at one of the region's many parks. "I don't know, madam," he replied. "I've only been here 11 years."

Abbey worked at Arches National Park, the site of the world's largest concentration of natural arches and one of the two most popular national parks in the region. The other is Canyonlands, where the Green and Colorado Rivers converge in a labyrinth of canyons.

The U.S. Bureau of Land Management, U.S. Forest Service, and state of Utah also control several million acres in the region. Not only are these lands just as spectacular as the nearby national parks, they also have fewer restrictions on public use. On most BLM lands, for example, visitors can camp, climb, drive, and bicycle just about anywhere.

In the 1980s, the area's largest community, Moab (pop. 5,000), began a nationwide campaign to attract tourists. The effort was an overwhelming success, and today Moab is a mecca for mountain bikers, four-wheel-drive enthusiasts, hikers, and river rafters from around the world. Spring break— March and April—is an especially busy time: Moab hosts a jeep safari during which more than 10,000 four-wheel-drive enthusiasts converge on the town.

"We went fishing for a little tourism and hooked a great white shark," says Bill Hedden, a commissioner on the Grand County Council.

Hedden remembers the time he'd had enough: Easter weekend 1993. Tents dotted the landscape around Moab as if a great army were bivouacking. Residents had to wait until midnight to avoid hour-long waits in check-out lines at the grocery store. Columns of four-wheel-drive vehicles and mountain bikes tied up traffic, blocked roads, and raced across the terrain. A conflict between four-wheelers and mountain bikers erupted into a full-fledged riot. People fought, fired guns, and even chased off a sheriff's posse. Even worse was the damage inflicted upon the land. Rioters uprooted centuries-old pinyon and juniper trees and burned them in bonfires. At a nearby archeological site, a group tore the roof beams out of an ancient cliff dwelling so they could build a fire to roast hot dogs. "We're talking about turning this country into rocks and dirt," Hedden says.

*Overwhelmed by tourism, Moab, Utah, leaders are now working with public land managers to manage visitation and restore damaged areas. Funding comes from a new user fee assessed on campers and mountain bikers. (Robert Glenn Ketchum)*

The only good thing about the riot was that it happened to coincide with a meeting of federal land managers in Moab. Officials saw firsthand the problems that result when county, state, and federal managers don't cooperate on issues that span jurisdictional boundaries. Their solution was the Canyon Country Partnership, an alliance of commissioners from four counties (Carbon, Emery, Grand, and San Juan); federal officials from the BLM, U.S. Forest Service, and National Park Service; and officials from three different state agencies. The Partnership's mission is to protect the region's natural ecosystems, while furthering local and regional objectives. "The partners share information and work together to assure that individual decisions make collective sense for the land and the community," says Hedden.

Much of the Partnership's work focuses on controlling the damaging side-effects of heavy recreational use. Number one on the agenda is a regional recreation management strategy to deal with spring break crowds. Already, the BLM, the state, and Grand County have agreed to jointly manage a heavily used recreation area, BLM's Sand Flats, on the outskirts of Moab. Sand Flats is home to Moab's most popular attraction, the Slickrock Bicycle Trail, which was the site of the 1993 riots.

To prevent future problems at Sand Flats, the Partnership got help from AmeriCorps, a national service program that provides work for young adults. A 10-person AmeriCorps crew installed toilets and waste bins in Sand Flats and closed off unauthorized trails and roads. AmeriCorps is also restoring denuded areas and educating mountain bikers and four-wheelers about the importance of staying on roads and trails. The Canyon Country Partnership recently published a "leave-no-trace" camping guide, which the AmeriCorps crew distributes free to all visitors.

To offset the cost of their projects, AmeriCorps is collecting entrance fees from Sand Flats users: $3 for vehicles, $1 for bicyclists, and $4 for overnight camping. The fee is generating between $10,000 and $20,000 a month, all of which goes into a county fund that supports on-the-ground improvements and law enforcement at Sand Flats. "All the money stays here," says Craig Bigler, who oversees the AmeriCorps crew.

The Partnership is working to improve land management at other sites in the region, too. Federal, state, and county agencies are making sure that all their data and information are recorded in the same form. And BLM and the state are talking about exchanging scattered parcels of land so that they can consolidate their holdings to reduce management problems.

Commissioner Hedden cautions that collaborative efforts will succeed only when participants want to work together. "You can't legislate partnerships," he says. But when everyone stands to gain, together they can accomplish a great deal more than an individual agency or group working alone.

## Case Study

# Estes Park, Colorado

*Rocky Mountain National Park, Colorado, may be the best place in the United States to catch a glimpse of a bighorn sheep or to hear the high-pitched bugle of a bull elk. The park's magnificent wildlife won't survive, however, if residential development of private lands along the park boundary continues to disrupt long-used migration routes to wintering areas. In Estes Park, the eastern gateway to the park, residents and local officials have teamed up to preserve private lands important to the area's wildlife. In 1995, voters in Larimer County, which lies north and east of the park and includes Estes Park, approved a county-wide 0.25 percent sales tax to finance open-space acquisition.*

Estes Park may not be the highest city in the United States, but it's an awfully strong contender. Tucked in an alpine valley at the foot of the Rocky Mountains, the city stands at more than 7,800 feet above sea level. With the snow-capped peaks of the Rockies glimmering high above town, residents here live in a world most Americans see only on postcards.

Estes Park is the eastern gateway to Rocky Mountain National Park. Established in 1915, the park protects the highest peaks of the Colorado Front Range. Within its boundaries lie 113 summits higher than 10,000 feet; one-third of the 266,000-acre park is above tree line.

Like many gateway communities, Estes Park depends on a heavy flow of tourists. Dozens of souvenir shops, motels, and restaurants line the town's streets, each hoping to snare some of the three million people who visit the park each year. "We all complain about the droves of tourists every summer," says Tim Phillips, who manages the local McDonald's, "but three-quarters of the businesses here couldn't survive without the park."

Estes Park has been "discovered": During the 1980s, the population here grew by more than 35 percent. Luring newcomers is the town's high quality of life: striking mountain scenery, a virtually nonexistent crime rate, and a friendly atmosphere where strangers exchange hellos. Most people don't move here for a job but instead bring their livelihood with them. Many use fax machines, overnight mail, and computer modems to communicate with offices and clients in Denver or Los Angeles. For others, a monthly dividend or retirement check will find them regardless of where they live.

The park is a leading factor in the town's growth. Although much of the park is bordered by national forest land, a substantial portion—about 37 percent—abuts private property. Private land adjacent to the park is prized for homesites, since the lots come with a seemingly endless backyard that's not only pristine but permanently protected as well. Who wouldn't want to live next to a national park?

*In Estes Park, Colorado, new homes rise along the boundary of Rocky Mountain National Park. Because the park contains relatively little wintering habitat, land adjacent to the park must be preserved if healthy populations of wildlife are to be maintained. Larimer County recently approved a 0.25 percent sales tax to finance open-space acquisition; Estes Park leaders are now working with national park officials to identify the top priorities for acquisition. (Ed McMahon)*

Unfortunately, the surge in real estate development adjacent to the park is beginning to affect the park's resources. Because the park itself contains relatively few of the low-altitude meadows and bottomlands that wildlife needs to survive the harsh Colorado winter, the park's largest mammals—bighorn sheep, elk, mule deer, and moose—frequently drift back and forth between the park and the lower elevation lands that surround it. Many of these surrounding meadows—as well as the migration corridors to them—are the very same lands commanding steep prices on the Estes Park real estate market. "Open spaces that just a few years ago were major wintering habitat are now developed," says Park Superintendent Homer Rouse.

Private development of wintering habitat and migration corridors can be deadly for wildlife. In the winter, the park's large ungulates need habitat that offers easy-to-find forage and limits exposure to biting winds. High-quality wintering habitat adjacent to the park must be preserved if healthy populations of wildlife are to be found in the park. "This park doesn't contain a complete ecosystem," says Rouse. "We're inextricably linked with the lands on our borders."

Already, there is evidence that development along the park boundary is taking its toll. In the winter of 1994, a contagious strain of viral pneumonia killed more than 70 of the 100 bighorn sheep found in the Estes Park area. Gene Schoonveld of the Colorado Division of Wildlife believes that development of lands adjacent to the park contributed to the spread of the disease by reducing available range and concentrating animals in remaining wintering habitat. Stress caused by more frequent interactions with humans and pets also makes the animals more susceptible to disease. "There's no question development played a role in the outbreak," Schoonveld says.

Rapid development also detracts from Estes Park's breathtaking alpine scenery, which is the reason many people live here. Views from Trail Ridge Road, which traverses the park and climbs to more than 12,000 feet, once showcased a landscape untouched by human hands. Recent developments adjacent to the park boundary, however, have marred vistas from overlooks on the eastern edge of the park, and condominiums and road cuts along the boundary are clearly visible from several rest stops and campgrounds. "We're destroying the very thing we all came for," says Tim Phillips, the McDonald's manager.

Alarmed by its rapid growth, Estes Park recently began a community-planning process designed to produce a new land-use plan for the town and valley. Twenty-eight "visioning" workshops were held in the fall of 1993; more than 1,500 people voiced their ideas on what makes the Estes Valley special and what needs to be done to preserve the region's distinctive character.

Later that year, local leaders and the Park Service convened a two-day conference to explore cooperative approaches to resolving the land-use challenges confronting the region. Attendees included representatives from the towns of Estes Park and Grand Lake, county commissioners from the three counties that flank the park, landowners, homeowner associations, officials from the national park and other government agencies, university faculty, and local chambers of commerce, citizens groups, and environmental organizations.

Largely because of the discussions initiated at the workshop, in 1995 voters in Larimer County—which lies north and east of the park and includes Estes Park—approved a county-wide 0.25 percent sales tax to finance open-space acquisition. Approved by a two-to-one margin, the tax is expected to raise $6.2 million a year. A similar referendum failed in 1994, but this time proponents rewrote it so that communities within Larimer County receive a share of the proceeds. By law, at least 55 percent of the revenue will be distributed to localities; Estes Park, for example, should receive approximately $200,000 a year.

Meanwhile, officials at Rocky Mountain National Park are building partnerships with adjacent landowners and communities. "We realize we're not going to protect this park by standing on the boundary and looking inside," says Jim Mack, the chief naturalist for the park.

In 1992, the park hired a land-use specialist, Larry Gamble, whose principal job is to communicate the park's message to adjacent landowners and communities and build partnerships with local groups. Gamble meets regularly with town and county officials to discuss land-use strategies that steer development away from critical habitat areas and view sheds or encourage developers to cluster lots so that open space is a part of every project.

Gamble also has designed a brochure titled, *Hey, There's a National Park in My Backyard!*, which helps homeowners avoid activities that degrade the park's resources. Mailed to every landowner in Estes Park, the brochure suggests how sound property management can contribute to the park's integrity. Landscaping with native plants, leashing pets, and designing homes to harmonize with the landscape are just a few of the many suggestions in the brochure.

For cooperative strategies to work, Gamble says, the Park Service must look for ways to help the town. "If we're going to have any relationship with Estes Park, it's going to have to be a two-way street."

Several opportunities have been identified. For one, the Park Service could help Estes Park smooth out the seasonal fluctuations in its economy. The biggest complaint from Estes Park businesses is that visitors—and income—drop off sharply each September. Three-quarters of the park's visitation takes place during the summer months, forcing many Estes Park businesses to close their doors during the lengthy off-season. To shift summer visitation to other months, the Park Service could promote the park's attractiveness in the off-season, using brochures that highlight the park's golden groves of aspen in the fall or its cross-country skiing in the winter.

Transportation management also could be improved. During the summer, congestion at signal lights in town often ties up traffic for hours. According to Steve Stamey, director of Estes Park's community development office, the Park Service could alleviate these bottlenecks by operating a tram system that shuttles visitors to the park. This would also improve visitor perceptions of the park: No one likes to view a park from a bumper-to-bumper column of automobiles.

While it's still too early to predict success in Estes Park, the cooperative approach undertaken there clearly demonstrates that the community, the park, and private landowners can all benefit from working together. But park officials point out that action in Estes Park began only after a sincere effort by the park to assist the community with the unique land-use and economic problems it faces.

"Before we are going to succeed at convincing people to look out for resource interests, we need to do a more effective job at looking out for their economic interests," says Jim Mack, the park's naturalist. "Establishing the long-term connection that they are one and the same interest will be the turning point."

Case Study
===
## Mount Desert Island, Maine

*By definition, gateway communities possess relatively little private land. That means they often cast a wary eye at proposals that seek to expand public lands on their borders. In Mount Desert Island, however, local leaders have found that conservation easements can allow continued preservation of lands impor-tant to Acadia National Park yet accommodate local needs for affordable hous-ing, economic development, and property-tax revenue.*

For eight months of the year, the single traffic light on Mount Desert Island never has more than a few cars waiting for it to change. In the summer, though, the light controls an intersection that easily could be mistaken for the busy streets of downtown Boston.

Every year, more than three million people journey to Mount Desert Is-land to visit Acadia National Park, the first national park east of the Missis-sippi River. The attractions are Acadia's evergreen forests of pine and spruce, dozens of sparkling lakes and ponds, and lofty cliffs of ancient gran-ite rising up to take on the Atlantic. The submerged tip of a receding moun-tain range, Mount Desert Island also boasts the highest point on the east-ern seaboard, the 1,530-foot Cadillac Mountain. From its summit, the eye beholds an unparalleled view of the archipelago that dots the Maine coast like buoys in a harbor.

Residing here are an independent people who earn their living from the sea. "Men whose lives glided on like rivers that water the woodlands," Long-fellow wrote. Even today, a person listening to a conversation between two Mount Desert Island lobstermen will know the culture here developed with few outside influences.

While the seafood industry remains a vital part of the local economy, Mount Desert Island's principal livelihood is tourism. Since the late 1800s, America's most affluent and socially prominent families have "summered" on the island. When the conservation movement dawned at the turn of the century, many of these families donated their estates to the federal govern-ment. In 1916, the government set aside these lands as Acadia National Park, the first U.S. park—and one of the only parks—established entirely by donations of land.

*Much of the rugged coast of Mount Desert Island, Maine, is protected by Acadia National Park. A coalition of nonprofit organizations, park leaders, and local governments has found that conservation easements can help safeguard other important lands on the Island in a way that allows for continued economic development and private home ownership. (Ed McMahon)*

Unlike many parks, Acadia's holdings are scattered throughout the island like squares on a chessboard. "Acadia's unique in that it's not a distinct resource outside a town," says Heidi Beal, whose family has lived here for nearly 200 years. "The park is everywhere."

Although Acadia clearly sustains the local economy, many residents blame it for the onslaught of summer tourists. Parking shortages and traffic jams plague the area all season long. And forget about trying to eat at a local restaurant unless you make reservations well in advance. "It's a two-edged sword," says Pete Madeira, owner of the Harbor 5 & 10 Variety Store and manager of one of the island's lobster wholesalers. "The park is the heart of our economy, but it's also the source of all our congestion."

What's more, on an island where real estate is a precious commodity, every acre in the park means one less available for development and one less subject to local property taxes. With roughly half the island in public ownership, "there's an awful lot of land that we don't get any taxes on," says Ken Minier, manager of the town of Southwest Harbor.

Many also blame the park for skyrocketing housing costs. "Property values in the town of Mount Desert are high enough now so that it's impossible for local people to buy a home," says Dave Irvin, who chairs the town planning board. "You can afford the lot or the house, but not both."

Compounding the problem, Acadia until recently had no established boundaries and could be enlarged anytime someone wished to donate land. That changed in 1986, when Congress froze the park at 41,250 acres and prohibited any further expansion. "Before the boundary law, people were afraid they'd run out of land and eventually be forced off the island," says Paul Haertel, superintendent of Acadia since 1994. "That law put to rest a lot of concerns."

Although the 1986 law prohibits Acadia from adding land outside its newly drawn boundary, it does allow the Park Service to acquire conservation easements, which have become the park's most important tool for protecting critical lands on the island. The towns prefer them, too, since, unlike property owned wholly by the Park Service, lands under easement remain in private hands and on the tax rolls; only the development rights are acquired by the park. (Easements also can be structured to allow additional homes and buildings in prespecified areas.)

So far, Acadia has acquired 150 easements totaling about 6,000 acres; all but one of them have been donated. Most of the easements preserve undeveloped shorelines, nesting sites for bald eagles, or pristine watersheds vital to the local fishing industry. Fifty protect entire islands in the waters surrounding Acadia.

The Maine Coast Heritage Trust, a nonprofit conservation organization based on the island, has helped negotiate each of the easements. The trust serves as an independent party with which both sides can bargain. "We've found that a lot of landowners may want to protect their property but don't want to deal with the federal government," says the trust's David MacDonald. "They're more comfortable with us because they know someone on our board or have read our literature and information on private-land conservation tools."

The trust recently launched its own easement program to reach landowners with property that lacks the stunning views or significant resources that interest the park. These include smaller parcels like the one that allows a Maine family to retain a homestead held since the 18th century or another that ensures a pond will continue to host ice skaters every winter. So far, the trust has accepted 12 easements totaling more than 2,000 acres. "In a few decades, the only open spaces left on Mount Desert Island are going to be in the park or the ones we have easements on," says MacDonald.

Friends of Acadia is another local organization that helps protect quality of life on the island. Founded in 1986, Friends works for the continued protection of the park and to involve citizens in park management issues. Friends recently teamed up with the park to restore Acadia's "carriage roads," a 57-mile network of gravel byways that links some of the more popular sites in the park. According to Heidi Beal, project director for Friends, the carriage roads were constructed by the John D. Rockefeller Jr. family beginning in 1913 and are open to all uses except motor vehicles.

Friends of Acadia now hopes to unite residents of the island behind a vision for the future. Ken Olson, the organization's president, says, "Getting everyone behind a unified vision offers the most benefit to both the park and the communities on the island."

Achieving a common vision for the future will be difficult on an island where independence is prized. "Right now, the island has four different police departments and four different fire departments," says Dave Irvin. "It took us 20 years to get a regional high school." Still, proponents can take heart in that cooperation is beginning to occur. For the past several years, the island's four town managers have met once a month with the park superintendent to discuss issues of concern. "Sometimes it takes gallons of coffee and interminable patience," Haertel says, "but until you have that dialogue you're not going to make any real progress."

Dana Reed, town manager of Bar Harbor, agrees: "When town officials have a problem with the park, we no longer just snipe at them. We discuss it with park staff and try to arrive at a solution together."

In its short existence, the "League of Towns" has compiled baseline data on the island's water quality and developed jointly operated transfer stations to deal with recycling and solid-waste disposal. With a few successes under its belt, the League in 1996 hired a transportation consultant to identify areas of congestion and design a transit system to serve the whole island. "We have problems with people parking on the roadsides, parking anywhere there's space for their car," says Jerry Storey, manager of the town of Mount Desert. "We're coming to the point where we'll have to say, 'This place is full, please move on.'" Acadia stands ready to help. "The park can accommodate a lot of people," says Haertel. "It can't accommodate a lot of cars."

The park also has worked with individual towns. In 1994, the park and Mount Desert convened a "conservation easement study group" to discuss the park's policy of acquiring conservation easements on private lands. Many local people feared that easement acquisitions were making it difficult for residents to find affordable housing. A panel of town officials, park staff, landowners, and representatives from Friends of Acadia and the Maine Coast Heritage Trust eventually agreed that future easements will seek to protect only what needs to be protected, thereby reserving developable sites for future building. The group also agreed to begin publicizing the many benefits that conservation easements provide to the island—open space, recreation, and watershed protection, to name just a few.

Nonetheless, many residents feel that without limits on the number of people who can visit the island, increasing visitation will erode any gains made in managing traffic, keeping housing affordable, or providing visitors with a meaningful experience. "Nothing can expand indefinitely," says Dave Irvin. "To the extent that we can agree to grow to a certain size, be happy with that size, and stick to that size . . . well, that's going to be our measure of success."

## Recognize the Role of Nongovernmental Organizations

Every gateway community can benefit from local citizens groups that are informed, active, and capable of a sustained effort to oversee and carry out local initiatives. Most communities already have several such groups working on issues that they consider most important to local well-being. Typically, these groups concentrate on their specific mission with little regard for other issues affecting the community. An economic development council, for example, probably isn't going to concern itself with securing public access to a local river, nor is a local conservation organization likely to become involved in bringing new businesses to town.

In the gateway communities most successful at dealing with growth, one organization has transcended its traditional role or mission and focused instead on convincing local people to take on the entire range of issues important to the community. By reaching out and moving beyond single-issue advocacy, this group is able to unite the community behind shared priorities.

In our experience, these types of groups have included economic development councils, chambers of commerce, neighborhood groups, local chapters of the League of Women Voters, senior citizens associations, or local environmental organizations. Some of these groups actually implement the community's ideas and initiatives, others provide a forum where citizens can discuss options and exchange ideas. All place a high value on public involvement.

Whatever its approach, an organization that addresses all of a community's priorities—from affordable housing to wildlife conservation to weekend activities for teenagers—will find it easier to win support for its objectives. Here are a few examples of community groups that have benefited from looking out for the broader interests of the community:

• The Malpai Borderlands Group is a nonprofit organization of ranchers, conservationists from The Nature Conservancy, and government land managers working to maintain ranching and preserve open space in the boot heel of New Mexico and the southeastern corner of Arizona, a region that encompasses nearly one million acres. Despite their varied backgrounds, Mal-

*The Malpai Borderlands Group is a nonprofit organization of ranchers, representatives from The Nature Conservancy, and government land managers working to maintain ranching and preserve open space in the boot heel of New Mexico and the southeastern corner of Arizona. Despite their varied backgrounds, Malpai group members have found common ground in a concern for promoting healthy, unbroken grasslands. (Jay Dusard)*

pai group members have found common ground in a concern for promoting healthy, unbroken grasslands. Because the region remains as open rangeland, with few houses or second homes, group members rely on regular burning—a common occurrence on the landscape before settlement—to keep trees from invading. It takes three to six years for a burned area to recover, however, so ranchers need a place for their stock to graze until the grasses come back. With money from grants and donations, the Malpai Borderlands Group purchases forage from the largest ranch in the area, the 500-square-mile Gray Ranch, then offers it to ranchers in areas recovering from a burn. As an incentive to keep the Malpai region as open rangeland, ranchers who establish a conservation easement on their ranch receive the forage for free. So far, four ranchers have agreed to conservation easements, ensuring that ranching remains a cog in the local economy and protecting the region's landscape.

• Spanning an area from southeast Arizona to the Colorado River Delta, the U.S.–Mexico border region of the Sonoran Desert is considered one of the world's largest intact arid ecosystems. Much of it is in public ownership:

On the United States side of the border are Cabeza Prieta National Wildlife Refuge and Organ Pipe Cactus National Monument; in Mexico are the Pinacate and Upper Gulf of California biosphere reserves. Since 1992, the International Sonoran Desert Alliance, a nonprofit citizens group, has worked to safeguard the region's resources and promote appropriate economic activities. Board members include citizens of the U.S., Mexico, and the Tohono O'odham and Cucupa tribes. In its short existence, the alliance has developed an environmental education program for school children, made it easier for local residents to avoid border-crossing disputes, and helped improve public participation in federal land management. Priorities and strategies are determined through monthly meetings open to all comers. "This organization is successful because it addresses not just one issue," says board member Lorraine Eiler, "but the whole spectrum of issues important to residents here."

• As the gateway to four of the East Coast's largest national wildlife refuges, Tyrrell County, North Carolina, is well positioned to benefit from tourism. Since 1992, the Tyrrell County Community Development Corporation has worked to see that local residents have the skills and expertise needed to open and operate new businesses like restaurants, bed and breakfasts, and retail stores. One of the corporation's first tasks was to identify job opportunities for the region's 18- to 25-year-olds. This led to creation of a local Youth Conservation Corps, in which teenagers and young adults spend four days a week in job training and community service projects, with the fifth day devoted to completing school or pursuing a higher degree. Each corps member receives a stipend. At the same time, the organization wants to make sure that economic gains don't come at the expense of the natural resources responsible for growth in the first place. With assistance from the University of North Carolina, the corporation is preparing a comprehensive development plan for the county that identifies economic options compatible with the region's wetland environment.

• The rolling pastures and meadows of Marin County, California, provide a scenic gateway to Point Reyes National Seashore. From 1950 to 1980, however, the county lost half of its farms and ranches as owners abandoned agricultural operations due to rising estate taxes, the high cost of expanding, or attractive offers from developers. In 1980, a group of farmers and other residents, fearful of losing the area's rural character, decided to create a nonprofit organization to acquire conservation easements in voluntary transactions with farmers and ranchers. By doing so, the Marin Agricultural Land Trust (better known as MALT) not only preserves the county's way of life, it also helps keep agriculture part of the local economy. (Marin County's farms contribute $50 million a year to the economy.) All told, MALT has purchased or received donations of easements on more than 25,000 acres of farm and ranch land throughout the county. MALT has paid from $350 to $1,000 an acre for the easements it has acquired, or between 25 and 50 percent of average property values in Marin County. The organization is funded by two local foundations and by a state bond act that in 1988 provided it with $15 million.

• In Washington State, the Willapa Alliance is a citizens group working to improve the quality of the local environment and implement economic development strategies that won't degrade the ecology and traditional way of life along Willapa Bay. A coalition of local residents, landowners, and members of the Shoalwater Bay Indian Tribe, the alliance promotes better understanding of ecological issues, enhances communication among residents, and champions local businesses and enterprises that add value to locally produced natural resources. With help from a regional conservation group, EcoTrust, the alliance has provided Willapa Bay residents with business skills, access to markets and credit, and the financial capital needed by fledgling enterprises. By restoring salmon habitat and promoting sustainable fishing, the group also is making sure that the Willapa Bay watershed remains healthy. Public education and involvement are cornerstones of the effort.

• In eastern Idaho, the Teton County Economic Development Council is leading efforts to find economic development options that complement the rural qualities of the growing Teton Valley. In 1991, the council sponsored a day-long visioning workshop where valley residents overwhelmingly approved maintaining the valley's rural nature, promoting a healthy agricultural community, and stemming the loss of open space. Since then, the council has worked solely on projects to realize that vision. It has raised money for local initiatives to keep farming healthy, sponsored training seminars for the county's small businesses, and helped market locally produced products. The council's top priority is to attract investors for a new Teton Valley gourmet cheese factory, which will purchase the entire milk output of the area's 25 dairy farmers and produce specialty cheeses, dips, and salad dressings. "The key to preserving our quality of life is to keep local agriculture and businesses healthy," says Dick Clark, the council's chairman.

• Blessed by a beautiful climate and abundant open lands, including the Colorado National Monument and Uncompahgre, Manti-LaSal, and Grand Mesa National Forests, Mesa County, Colorado, is one of the fastest growing regions in the state. Many of Mesa County's orchards—which produce 75 percent of the state's peaches—are being bulldozed to make room for new homes. Soaring real estate prices have also made it difficult for young farmers to take over family farms. Since 1980, the Mesa County Land Conservancy has worked to keep agriculture a healthy component in the local economy and preserve the region's open space. Founded by local farmers, the conservancy's strategy is to inform farmers and ranchers about voluntary land-conservation tools. The conservancy then accepts donations of conservation easements from owners who want to protect their land and make sure it remains in production. More than 4,500 acres have been protected. "Agriculture has been a vibrant and stable part of Mesa County's economy through boom and bust," says conservancy staff member Anne Landman. "We don't want it to disappear. Remember: Orange County, California, used to be all orange trees."

• In northern New York, the Champlain Valley Heritage Network is pursuing cooperative efforts to boost the economies and preserve the rural landscape of nine communities between the Adirondack Mountains and Lake Champlain. The network is a diverse coalition of local chambers of commerce, business owners, farmers, bed and breakfasts, and government officials. First and foremost, the group hopes to preserve the area's rural lifestyle by raising the income of local farmers. It has helped farmers garner more for their products by increasing consumer awareness of the Champlain Valley, much as maple syrup from Vermont seems to command a higher price than syrup from other states. The group also supported the state's purchase in 1994 of a lakefront estate that was likely headed for residential subdivision. The state agreed to the network's condition that farmland on the parcel remain under cultivation. Tourism is another strategy. With assistance from the state and the nonprofit Countryside Institute, the network has produced a colorful map and guide featuring diagrams of each community and local points of interest, including museums, historic sites, golf courses, nature walks, boat launches, recreation areas, fishing hot spots, and annual events and festivals. Each community has erected interpretive signs that tie in with the map. "We want to attract economic development," says Ron Ofner, director of the Essex County tourism bureau, "but in a way that doesn't ruin what we have here."

## Case Study

# Red Lodge, Montana

*Overcoming apathy is a constant struggle for many communities. Ironically, one way to defeat it is to delegate responsibility for action directly to citizens, who often respond with impressive results. In Red Lodge, citizen-based task forces—working with little resources other than their own time and effort—set up a fully staffed Boys and Girls Club for local youths, established a water-quality monitoring program for the city's water supply, and helped enact a new land-use plan for their community. Red Lodge proves that, once enthused and empowered, citizens are quite capable of taking the reins.*

Montana is often referred to as "the last best place." Nowhere is this more accurate than in Red Lodge, a friendly community of 2,000 people in the shadow of the Rocky Mountains. Red Lodge is a gateway to one of the premier wilderness areas in the Lower 48, the Absaroka–Beartooth Mountains, where you can still hear the howl of a wolf and the roar of a grizzly bear. The city also is surrounded by working ranches and irrigated meadows, which accentuate its feel as a gateway community.

Red Lodge marks the beginning of the Beartooth Scenic Highway, a 69-mile two-lane road that winds its way up to nearly 11,000 feet before depositing travelers at the northeastern entrance to Yellowstone National Park. Charles Kuralt called it "the most beautiful drive in America." Red Lodge was once a mining town. Around the turn of the century, immigrants from

*Nestled in a mountain valley, Red Lodge, Montana, is a gateway to one of the premier wilderness areas in the continental U.S., the Absaroka–Beartooth Mountains. Residents have set up a number of citizen-based task forces to make sure the city doesn't lose its rural surroundings and small-town values. (Merv Coleman)*

Europe flocked here to mine coal for the locomotives of the Great Northern Railroad. In 1911, the city had more than 5,000 residents. Red Lodge's past remains evident downtown, where nearly every building makes an appearance on the National Register of Historic Places.

Today the mines are silent, but Red Lodge boasts a vibrant economy with a downtown commercial district fueled by tourism rather than coal. Spring, summer, and fall bring tourists on their way to Yellowstone and eager to explore the city. One of Red Lodge's biggest draws is the "Festival of Nations," a 10-day celebration in August featuring the music, cuisine, and culture of the city's many ethnic groups. In the winter, the action shifts to Red Lodge Mountain, which has a well-deserved reputation as one of the West's friendliest downhill ski resorts.

Like other communities in scenic areas, Red Lodge is changing. Retirees and baby boomers in search of the good life are moving here in droves. Between 1988 and 1993, rental costs in Red Lodge doubled, while housing prices increased 170 percent. Besides higher housing costs, newcomers also bring new values. Downtown, brightly painted buildings clash with traditional building styles, while outside the city newly built homes occupy what was once prime rangeland, threatening the ranching industry with the same fate that befell the coal mines.

To meet these challenges head on, in 1992 the citizens of Red Lodge gathered for a two-day workshop—termed the Beartooth Front Community Forum—to discuss their city's future. Participants first sought a consensus on what makes Red Lodge such a good place to live. Leading vote getters were the city's western history and architecture, recreational opportunities, mountain views, and cultural diversity. Above all, residents prized the city's small town values and neighborly atmosphere. "Only in Red Lodge can you end up having a conversation with a wrong number," is how one participant put it.

Before the workshop adjourned, citizens had identified a number of projects to help Red Lodge retain its high quality of life. "In a lot of ways, the workshop was like a revival tent," says resident John Clayton. "We went in and we came out ready to go to work."

And work they did. Several citizen-based task forces—with membership open to any resident of the area—were set up to explore the issues participants deemed most important. Task forces first came up with ideas on how to make Red Lodge a better place for youths and senior citizens. An arts and recreation committee helped lay the groundwork for a new Boys and Girls Club for children between the ages of 6 and 14. With donations from residents, an executive director was hired in June 1994 and the club opened for business just two years after it was first proposed. Today the club serves more than 235 children.

Another task force examined ways for the city to maintain its environmental quality through private-sector initiatives. Its first project was a water-testing program for Rock Creek, the city's source of drinking water. The panel raised $3,000 to purchase testing kits then recruited several volunteers to conduct regular monitoring. "We're out there every month," says volunteer Jim Coates, "except in the winter, when we can't get to the water."

This same task force also invited Red Lodge landowners to a briefing on conservation easements and other private conservation tools. Within a year of the briefing, three local ranchers donated conservation easements on more than 10,000 acres of working ranchland. "That meeting planted the seed in the minds of those landowners," says Bill Long of the Montana Land Reliance, which holds the easements. "At the very least, it poured water on a few seeds already in the ground." The easements not only assure that ranching will remain a part of the local economy, they also help maintain the open lands on Red Lodge's fringes.

A separate task force was set up to make sure Red Lodge didn't lose the momentum generated by the workshop. This committee eventually created a new citizen-based nonprofit organization, the Beartooth Front Corporation, to plan meetings and events and make sure Red Lodge citizens stay active in local decisions. "It takes a constant effort, but you have to involve people who may be disinclined to participate," says resident Gary Ferguson, a writer and former Forest Service ranger. "If they're not there, you have to find ways to get them there."

The group's regular meetings often begin with guest speakers who discuss community projects, provide briefings on state laws or local economic trends, or share a little of Red Lodge's history. Popular speakers also can attract people who may not otherwise show up. "One time to get ranchers to come to a meeting," says Ferguson, "our guest speaker was the head of a regional agricultural network who is a favorite television personality among farmers and ranchers."

Another task force was charged with examining government land-use planning efforts. After reviewing efforts in other communities, the task force concluded that a land-use plan could help convert the wishes of Red Lodge citizens into a blueprint for the future, but that the city first needed a professional to inventory the area's resources and help prepare a valid plan.

In 1994, with that recommendation in mind, and with funds from both the city budget and private donations, the Red Lodge City Council hired a certified planner, Lee Nellis, with a reputation of helping small towns prepare for the future. "The land-use planner was not hired to tell our community what to do," reads one of the group's newsletters. "He was employed to help us turn raw data into a clear picture of existing growth trends, to share problem-solving techniques that other rural communities have found useful, and to help us navigate a maze of legal do's and don'ts."

The group organized several forums where Nellis could field questions from residents, discuss planning issues, and allow residents to share their views about Red Lodge's needs. Even developers approved of the planning process. "I wasn't a fan of it in the beginning," says Ron Wolfe, "but the process has helped by letting me know what I can do with my land. Some of my land will be more valuable as a result."

Largely because of the committee's efforts to involve citizens in the planning process, the Red Lodge City Council in 1995 voted unanimously to implement the new citizen-designed master plan, which addresses everything from economics to aesthetics. To encourage new industries to locate to Red Lodge, the plan designates a new light-industrial park on the edge of the city. "People want to make sure there are some real jobs that aren't tourism related," says Nellis. "Without the industrial park, there's no place left to put a small industrial operation."

The plan also calls for land acquisition and landscaping projects to keep the entrances to the community attractive. A new design-review panel will prevent unsightly buildings and uphold Red Lodge's western architectural traditions. And a city planning board now has responsibility for reviewing projects and making recommendations to the city council. In the past, such reviews were handled by a county-level board. "A city planning board will be much more focused, since they'll have responsibility for just Red Lodge and not the whole county," says Gary Ferguson.

The citizens of Red Lodge aren't done yet. New task forces are investigating ways to promote affordable housing, encourage sustainable businesses to locate to the area, develop a new "assisted-living" facility for Red Lodge's senior citizens, and create a new youth center for older teens. "In the past, Red Lodge just elected people and let them make the decisions," says City Councilwoman Renee Tafoya. "Now, people here are making the decisions themselves."

In 1994, the sense of empowerment engendered by the forums helped Red Lodge achieve one of its biggest accomplishments: keeping the local post office downtown. Claiming its old facility was outdated, the U.S. Postal Service proposed to abandon its downtown post office and build a "modern" one on the outskirts of town. Like many rural communities, Red Lodge has no residential mail delivery; instead every resident has a box at the post office. "Picking up the mail is a social event where you can catch up with your neighbors," says John Clayton.

Although the Postal Service wanted a facility more accessible to delivery trucks, moving the office from downtown meant that most residents would have to drive to get their mail. For many of the town's senior citizens, this spelled the end of social trips to the post office. Instead of accepting the Postal Service's decision, Red Lodge citizens launched a campaign to persuade their congressman, Rep. Pat Williams, to strike funding for the new

*Red Lodge citizens have found ways to preserve historic buildings and maintain the city's pedestrian-friendly downtown. New priorities are to attract sustainable businesses and establish a senior citizens center. (Merv Coleman)*

post office from the Postal Service's budget. The grassroots lobbying effort worked, and while the post office has moved to a larger building, it's still located downtown.

"A couple of years earlier, we wouldn't have had the confidence to do what we did with the post office," says Ferguson. "Now everyone thinks, 'Hey, there's a problem—let's see what we can do about it.'"

## Provide Opportunities for Leaders to Step Forward

Another trait shared by the gateway communities most successful at shaping growth to their liking is that individual citizens often become more than just participants. A few local leaders have made significant differences in the well-being of their communities. Sometimes these people are longtime residents upset with how unmanaged growth has changed what they love about their home. Or they might be newcomers who want to make sure that their adopted hometown doesn't develop the same ugliness or congestion as the one they left. More often than not, they're simply citizens who care a great deal about their community.

All too often, people conclude that they can't change the course of events in their community. In our experience, however, everyday people—not just politicians or "experts"—can and do make a difference. The challenge is to provide opportunities for new leaders to step forward and get involved. In a number of gateway communities, the citizens who spearheaded campaigns to improve their town wouldn't have emerged if the community hadn't given them a chance to participate.

Even a community group or public agency with the best of intentions can unwittingly develop a closed decision-making process that makes it difficult for local people to get involved. Leadership training and development thus should be crucial elements of any community organization or local government. "Allowing leaders to come forward is one of the most critical things a community or group can do," says Meriwether Jones of the Aspen Institute.

Here are a few examples of people who have made a difference in their communities:

• Almost single-handedly, conservationist Jerry Adelmann created the Illinois and Michigan Canal National Heritage Corridor, a linear park that stretches for 120 miles along an abandoned canal linking Chicago with the Mississippi River system. Adelmann's success at building local support for the park convinced Congress in 1984 to add the canal corridor to the national park system. Unlike most national parks, the I & M Canal has no federal holdings. Instead, it's a collection of local and state parks and privately owned buildings: 41 towns, 39 nature preserves, and 200 historic sites along the waterway. The national heritage corridor designation has helped revital-

*Jerry Adelmann recognized the economic and recreation potential of an abandoned canal along the Illinois River. Because of his efforts, the Illinois and Michigan Canal National Heritage Corridor is now an important asset to the communities it links. (Robert Cascarelli)*

ize the region's economy: Old steel mills and factories along the canal have been converted to offices, shops, and restaurants all marketed on the basis of their access to historic locks and trails. By helping safeguard the region's heritage, Adelmann initiated a new wave of economic growth and provided a model for partnerships among communities, states, and federal agencies.

• Citizen activists Betty Rankin and Annie Snyder spearheaded local efforts to stop a proposed supermall adjacent to Manassas National Battlefield Park, Virginia, where more than 22,000 Union and Confederate soldiers lost their lives in two Civil War battles. In January 1988, local officials, without receiving any public input, approved plans for a regional shopping mall and office complex next to the battlefield. Rankin and Snyder immediately formed the Save the Battlefield Coalition. At first the coalition was composed of Civil War enthusiasts, conservationists, veterans groups, and landowners from the area; however it soon grew to include people from all over the country. To raise money, the coalition held fund-raising events and sold bumper stickers, buttons, and t-shirts. They also took their campaign national, distributing press releases and staging well-publicized events. Largely because of Rankin, Snyder, and the coalition, Congress in 1988 added the entire property to the park. "It wasn't a matter of people not wanting growth," Rankin says. "It was a matter of a mall being built on hallowed ground."

• Like many small towns, the principal asset of Delta, Colorado, a gateway to the Grand Mesa and Gunnison National Forests, is its quality of life. Since he moved here in 1966, Tom Huerkamp has fought to keep it that way. Huerkamp, owner of an office-supply store, has led a battle to keep the local hospital open; rounded up votes for a school-bond issue; created a small-business assistance center; helped establish a new county-level water system; raised $500,000 to acquire public fishing access to the Gunnison River, one of the state's top trout streams; and twice successfully led opposition to a proposed state prison in the county. "Even with the jobs, the net effect of that prison would have been negative," he says. "It would have been visible from 40 miles away, on a site that's two-thirds of the way up one of the biggest mountains in the county and a prime wintering area for mule deer. Not to mention the stress it would have put on our schools, roads, law enforcement, the hospital—everything." Huerkamp believes rural communities are too quick to accept industries that appear to promise economic growth but, on closer inspection, might detract from local quality of life. "Communities need to be honest about their economic realities," he says. "The one thing we have here is a great lifestyle. The air's clean, the water's clean, there's very little crime, we're good neighbors. We need to be careful not to damage what we really value."

• Keith Lewis spends half his time at sea on merchant ships and half at home on Block Island, an 11-square-mile island off the Rhode Island coast. The island is home to more than 300 freshwater ponds and wetlands, as well as the Block Island National Wildlife Refuge, a narrow slice of sand dunes and beaches that provides a staging area for migratory waterfowl and shorebirds. A fifth-generation resident of Block Island, Lewis initiated efforts to prevent the island from becoming an exclusive community of summer homes. He donated his family farm to a local conservancy, creating the largest open-space preserve on the island. Then in 1985 he helped persuade Block Island's 600 full-time residents to impose a 2 percent transfer tax (later raised to 3 percent) on local real estate transactions. The tax revenue supports the Block Island Land Trust, a locally run group that acquires and manages open space. To win over residents worried that the tax would inflate the cost of housing, the tax was structured to exempt the first $75,000 of the purchase price of a primary residence bought by first-time homeowners. The land trust regularly surveys homeowners and residents to determine which properties merit protection. Nearly one-fifth of the island is now permanently protected.

• Larry Mann lives in Lexington, Virginia, a community of 7,000 people near the Blue Ridge Mountains. Lexington's most prominent geographic feature is House Mountain. When the largest private holding on the mountain was offered for sale, Mann visited the owners, expressed his concern about development on the mountain, and asked for a 90 day option to purchase the property. To his surprise, the family agreed. Mann quickly organized a citizens committee, Save House Mountain, which encouraged local citizens to buy the property for the community's benefit. "We reached out to everybody," he says. Mann's group raised more than half the $335,000 price tag, and a state agency—the Virginia Outdoors Foundation—agreed to finance the rest. Thanks to Mann's initiative and leadership, Lexington residents can continue to enjoy horseback riding, hunting, and hiking on House Mountain.

• Bob Sharp, a third-generation rancher in southeastern Arizona, refuses to let residential subdivision alter the ranching heritage of the San Rafael Valley, a 90,000-acre basin of pristine grassland ringed on three sides by the mountains of the Coronado National Forest and on the fourth by the U.S.–Mexico border. Sharp's tireless efforts to persuade local ranchers to

*Third-generation rancher Bob Sharp refuses to let residential subdivision alter the ranching heritage of Arizona's San Rafael Valley, shown here. Sharp's efforts to persuade his neighbors to prepare a framework for future land-use decisions paid off with the creation of a land trust that informs landowners of conservation options, accepts donations of land, and helps raise money to acquire interests in land. (Bob Sharp)*

prepare a framework for future land-use decisions finally paid off: In 1995, ranchers set up a new land trust—the San Rafael Valley Land Trust—that will keep ranching viable by guarding against subdivision of the valley's ranches. The trust informs landowners about conservation options, accepts donations of land, and helps raise money to acquire interests in land. Already, one landowner has reconsolidated several parcels that had been subdivided, and another has donated an agricultural preservation easement on a 450-acre ranch.

• In South Danbury, New Hampshire, Mary Lyn Ray's desire to protect the rural countryside near her home inspired her neighbors. In 1987, more than 155 acres of unbroken fields and woodlands surrounding Ray's home went on the market and appeared destined for development into small residential lots. "I knew immediately that I was going to buy the property and place a conservation easement on it," says Ray, an author of children's books.

"What I didn't know was how I would pay for it." Using sand and gravel deposits on the property as collateral, Ray arranged for a loan to purchase the land. When revenue from the gravel deposits fell short of the loan payments, Ray sold her collection of art and antiques and learned to make do on a shoestring budget. With her own land protected from development, Ray felt she could ask her neighbors to consider similar restrictions on their property. Under her leadership, more than 6,000 acres of forest and farmland in and around Danbury are now protected with conservation easements. "The citizens here have done something larger than they ever could have done on their own," she says.

• Land-use decisions on Sanibel Island, Florida, gateway to J.N. "Ding" Darling National Wildlife Refuge, were once made by county officials who ignored local concerns about Sanibel's escalating growth. In 1974, residents overwhelmingly approved a ballot measure to incorporate as the City of Sanibel and take control of their zoning and land-use decisions. A month later, a strong proponent of the ballot measure, Porter Goss, was elected as the city's first mayor. Goss's first project was a land-use plan based on the number of people Sanibel could sustain without affecting water quality, wildlife, and other natural features. Armed with this knowledge, Sanibel's city council approved a plan to protect sensitive areas and limit the number of building permits that can be awarded each year. Goss retired as mayor in 1980 but returned to action a year later when developers tried to overturn the plan. In a 1981 referendum, voters endorsed the plan by a three-to-one margin in an election that also put Porter Goss back in office. Goss now represents Sanibel Island in the U.S. House of Representatives.

• Jay Fetcher wanted to take over his family's ranch in the Upper Elk River Valley in Clark, Colorado, gateway to the Mt. Zirkel Wilderness Area. Doing so, however, would have required that he and his siblings subdivide and sell their property in order to pay the estate taxes. The family found an answer in conservation easements, which will allow them to reduce their estate-tax bill from $325,000 to zero, protect their ranch from development, and continue the family's ranching lifestyle. Although the family received no financial compensation for donating an easement, they retained an income source by setting aside sites for future development that won't interfere with ranching operations or detract from the valley's scenery. Together with neighbor Steve Stranahan, Fetcher has also convinced neighbors to begin protecting their ranches. Fetcher now travels around Colorado, talking to other ranchers about how conservation easements can help them stay on their land.

Case Study
=====

## The Sea Islands of Georgia and South Carolina

*Citizen input is only as good as the knowledge and expertise of the citizens themselves. In the Sea Islands of Georgia and South Carolina, where development pressures threaten one of the country's most distinctive cultures, an educational organization has dedicated itself to improving citizens' abilities to influence local decision making. By offering citizens training in leadership skills, problem solving, and land-use law, the Penn Center has helped Sea Island residents play a more prominent role in decisions about their future.*

Following the Civil War, the dozens of Sea Islands along the South Carolina and Georgia coast were one of the few areas in the South where land was made available for freed slaves. Thousands of newly freed slaves flocked to the islands and, isolated from the mainland, fused their African origins and American influences into a rich culture marked by a distinct cuisine, unique crafts, and a lilting dialect known as Gullah.

In the 1970s and 1980s, America's love affair with the ocean began to put an end to this isolation. Exclusive resorts with golf courses, private beaches, and jampacked marinas now dot the grassy marshes and moss-draped forests on many of the islands, displacing African-American communities more than a century old. Hilton Head, Fripp, and Kiawah islands, for example, have been transformed from isolated rural communities into bustling resorts. In the summer, more than 50,000 people a day crowd onto Hilton Head.

The newfound popularity of the Sea Islands has made it difficult for native islanders to retain land held for generations. Some developers have used "partition sales" to break up properties. Much of the land on the Sea Islands is owned in common by many relatives; by acquiring a single interest in such a property, a developer can force its sale then outbid other shareholders and acquire the entire tract of land. Escalating real estate values also have driven up property taxes, forcing many islanders to sell their property to meet tax liabilities.

The proliferation of resorts and retirement communities has also affected the traditional vocations of local people. Runoff from poorly planned development has decimated South Carolina's shellfish beds—more than half are now closed. And the art of basket weaving, a mainstay of the Sea Islands' culture, is now declining because development has cut off access to the "sweetgrasses" that grow in coastal wetlands.

Development threatens the Sea Islands' rich natural resources, too. On Hilton Head, for example, three-fourths of the natural wetlands have been lost to development, while 20 golf courses suck 250,000 gallons of water a day from the groundwater aquifer beneath the island. Several Sea Islands also lie amid the rich deltas of the Ashepoo, Combahee, and Edisto Rivers, which provide habitat for more than one-sixth of the waterfowl on the Atlantic Flyway.

Since the 1860s, the Penn Center has helped Sea Islanders receive an education and preserve their African-American culture. Founded by northern abolitionists, Penn Center is comprised of 19 buildings on a 50-acre campus on St. Helena Island, South Carolina. Today, the center's mission is to preserve the history, natural resources, and culture of the Sea Islands by training local officials, business leaders, and community members in civics, economic development, and natural resource conservation.

Every year the center conducts a six-month-long course where a select group of Sea Islanders devotes weekends to studying the challenges facing the region. Leadership skills are an essential part of the course. Penn Center's instructors help islanders learn how to hold effective meetings, conduct research, make presentations, negotiate, and arrive at consensus or group decisions.

Penn Center has also shown residents how estate planning can protect family lands from unscrupulous partition sales. Its workshops and one-on-one counseling sessions have reached thousands of Sea Island landowners. The center also has a sustainable development program that helps islanders find ways to prosper while retaining their culture and natural environment. A folk-art center teaches young adults languishing arts like basket weaving and quilt making then gives them a venue to sell their products to tourists. In another program, islanders are building a food-processing facility for locally grown produce and chartering a community development corporation to help local entrepreneurs get started.

In reality, the mission of the Penn Center—to give Sea Island residents the power to control their destiny—hasn't changed that much since Reconstruction. The difference is that today the center no longer teaches reading, writing, and arithmetic, but the more sophisticated skills that islanders need to protect their hard-fought gains.

## Pay Attention to Aesthetics

Throughout the country, many communities now review development proposals with an eye to protecting ecologically sensitive areas such as floodplains and wetlands. Even more promote orderly development that keeps local government investment in public facilities, services, and infrastructure to a minimum. The most successful communities, however, strive for development that is not only fiscally and environmentally sound, but visually pleasing as well.

"Aesthetic" amenities fall into two categories: the natural environment, which includes views of open space, mountains, or coastlines; and the "built" environment, which includes architecture, homes and buildings, signs, and other man-made creations. Protecting views and scenery is an increasingly important goal, and not just for cosmetic reasons. From coast to coast, communities are beginning to regard visual amenities as an integral part of their economic well-being. For instance, communities that pay attention to the elements that make their downtowns appealing—tree-lined streets, well-landscaped walkways, attractive signs, and historic façades—stand to gain more than just a handsome business district. Research shows that shoppers are more likely to patronize stores in commercial districts having an attractive and pedestrian-friendly environment.

Attractive design and landscaping also translate into a better financial return for landowners and developers. A 1994 study by the Urban Land Institute found that visual amenities added a sales or rental rate premium of at least 5 percent above the local market. And according to the National Association of Homebuilders, "Developed lots with trees sell for an average of 20–30 percent more than similarly sized lots without trees." Trees also can reduce runoff, substantially decreasing a project's stormwater management costs. Finally, attention to aesthetic features can help a project win support from local review boards or citizens groups.

In all cases, gateway communities should set an example by making their public property as attractive as possible. Public buildings and projects should demonstrate how development can be visually pleasing and compatible with local architectural traditions.

Here are a few examples of gateway communities that are paying attention to their visual amenities:

• Sedona, Arizona, a gateway to Oak Creek Canyon, one of Arizona's most popular attractions and a part of the Coconino National Forest, makes sure franchise architecture doesn't clash with its red-rock landscape. Incorporated as a city in 1988, Sedona has a rigorous design-review process that ensures that all franchise designs—including hotels, fast-food restaurants, and gas stations—are compatible with the community's unique setting and character.

• In Lander, Wyoming, gateway to the Wind River Range, the chamber of commerce invested in a downtown beautification campaign that refashioned the town's business district in the spirit of the Old West. Frontier-era

*The southwestern style of this McDonald's in Sedona, Arizona—complete with adobe walls and a teal-colored logo—blends in with the town's character. Many communities now realize that real estate development should not only be environmentally and fiscally sound, but visually pleasing, too. (Ed McMahon)*

trash receptacles and light posts line the streets, barrels of flowers adorn the curbs, and widened sidewalks beckon to pedestrians. The city also installed new park benches and bicycle racks. "There used to be empty storefronts throughout the downtown," says Paula McCormick, president of the Lander Area Chamber of Commerce. "Now it's hard to find a vacant building on Main Street." Local businesses are reaping the rewards. "Instead of just driving through," McCormick says, "people stop and say, 'This is a nice town, let's look around.'"

• Coral Gables, Florida, gateway to Biscayne National Park, offers commercial developers incentives that encourage Mediterranean designs compatible with the city's architectural style. Buildings with a Mediterranean flavor are awarded increased floor-to-area ratios, relaxed setback requirements, or additional building units.

• Hot Springs, Arkansas, has worked hand-in-hand with Hot Springs National Park to enhance the historic and visual character of the downtown districts that border the park's bathhouses. The city first designated a six-block historic district adjacent to the park; renovations of buildings within the district must meet historic preservation guidelines. More important, Hot Springs levied a temporary sales tax that raised $500,000 to help property owners restore their historic façades. The National Park Service and the state of Arkansas have contributed matching funds.

• Denver, Colorado, "gateway to the Rockies," has taken steps to protect views of the Rocky Mountains west of the city. The city established eight "view preservation areas," where the height of buildings is sharply restricted. The designations guarantee mountain views from the state capitol and from most city parks. Together, the designated areas cover 14 square miles, or about one-eighth of the city's land area.

• Dozens of gateway communities have banned billboards that block views and detract from scenery. Sun Valley, Idaho; Nags Head, North Carolina; Teton County, Wyoming; Provincetown, Massachusetts; and Sedona, Arizona, are some of the communities that prohibit billboards within their limits. Other gateway communities limit the size or number of billboards, ban new ones, or establish billboard-free districts. Many gateway communities also have guidelines specifying what signs can look like and how large they

*Many gateway communities have banned billboards to preserve scenic views like this one along a road in Sun Valley, Idaho. Others have restricted the size or number of signs, established billboard-free zones, or set up design committees to review new ones.(Ed McMahon)*

can be. The signs still transmit useful information, but without obstructing views or affecting character.

• Freeport, Maine, is known to millions of Americans as the home of mail-order retailer L.L. Bean. It's also the home of one of the country's most famous McDonald's restaurants. In 1982, McDonald's purchased a 130-year-old Victorian mansion in downtown Freeport and announced plans to demolish it and build a restaurant. Concerned that Freeport's local business district was becoming too commercial, citizens persuaded the city zoning board to require McDonald's to use the existing building. The restored house is now a dining area, while a one-level addition in back serves as the kitchen and serving counter. Freeport's McDonald's demonstrates that fast-food chains will comply with clear regulatory requirements.

• Two states—North Carolina and South Carolina—have enacted statewide laws to restrict the height of buildings constructed on mountain ridges. Known as Mountain Protection Acts, the laws preserve views of the Appalachian Mountains. Local officials and legislators endorsed the legislation because western Carolina's chief economic powers—tourism and second-home construction—depend on the visual integrity of mountains and ridge lines.

• To preserve views of the Flatiron Mountains, which provide a scenic backdrop for Boulder, Colorado, the city prohibits all buildings taller than 55 feet. In addition, special conditions apply to any buildings taller than 35 feet.

• Communities interested in retrofitting existing buildings or strip malls should visit Mashpee, Massachusetts, a town of about 7,000 people on Cape Cod. Mashpee decided to fashion a new town center out of an old shopping mall. Completed in 1986, the Mashpee Commons houses the town's post office, church, library, police and fire departments, and only grocery store, all within an easy walk of residential areas. Besides serving local residents, the Commons also draws from surrounding communities, making it a sound commercial investment.

• With help from a strong community group, Staunton, Virginia, now boasts one of the most attractive and vital downtowns of any city in Virginia. Since 1980, the Historic Staunton Foundation, a nonprofit organization, has offered free design assistance to any owner of a historic building in downtown Staunton. At first only a few owners made use of the foundation's advice. But after a few façades had been restored, the idea caught on and today almost every historic building in the city has been restored to its turn-of-the-century appearance. The result is a bustling downtown with restaurants, offices, one-of-a-kind shops, and apartments all housed in beautifully restored buildings.


Case Study
=====
# Fredericksburg, Virginia

*The most forward-thinking communities recognize that real estate development should not only be environmentally and fiscally sound, but visually pleasing as well. In Fredericksburg, city officials have worked with the National Park Service to ensure that real estate projects blend in with nationally significant Civil War battlefields. The city has also taken steps to preserve and restore the historic character of its downtown. For its part, the Park Service has provided guidance to local officials and grants to owners of historic buildings.*

Peaceful today, the rolling countryside surrounding Fredericksburg witnessed some of the fiercest fighting of the Civil War. Confederate and Union troops clashed here on four separate occasions; each time, General Robert E. Lee managed to turn back the invading Union army.

Fredericksburg and Spotsylvania National Military Park now preserves the sites of battles that claimed more than 100,000 lives. Created in 1927, the park is a patchwork of small, unconnected land holdings and linear strips of land that follow the trench lines and troop movements of the two armies. The park has few intact battlefields. "Only about half the land involved in the battles is actually protected by the park," says Superintendent George Church.

Population growth and sprawl have placed many park holdings in jeopardy. Only 50 miles from Washington, D.C., Spotsylvania County is one of Virginia's fastest growing counties, making the private lands adjacent to battlefields prime sites for commercial and residential development. Between 1980 and 1990, the county's population grew from 32,000 to 57,000, an increase of 79 percent. Many of the new residents are refugees from Washington: 25 percent of the workforce in Fredericksburg commutes to D.C., a drive of an hour-and-a-half each way.

Already, several Civil War sites in the county have been lost or degraded. Salem Church, for example, where Confederates holed up and held off an advancing army, is now surrounded not by Union troops but by a shopping mall, service station, and six-lane highway. And at the Wilderness battlefield, just 50 feet from a trench line used by Lt. General Richard Ewell's

*Confederate troops holed up in Salem Church in Fredericksburg, Virginia, to fend off an advancing Union army. Today, the church is surrounded not by Union troops, but by a shopping mall, service station, and six-lane highway. (National Park Service)*

Confederate corps, a dense thicket of oak, sweet gum, and hickory gives way to the manicured lawns of a residential subdivision. The trenches now guard the backyards and swing sets of suburban Fredericksburg.

In 1990, then-Superintendent Maria Burks concluded that the park's future depended on better relations with local landowners and officials. Under her direction, park officials set out to inventory the private land surrounding the park. They ultimately identified more than 70 "related sites" critical to interpreting the four battles.

Burks didn't stop there. The Park Service's previous efforts to influence development projects had failed, largely because park officials became involved too late in the process. Changing their approach, park officials began to demonstrate how the region's economic vitality is closely linked to the integrity of its historic buildings and battlefields. They cited statistics that show that ever since Ken Burns's PBS documentary on the Civil War, Americans have been visiting battlefields in record numbers.

Burks's economic-based arguments convinced the county that the Park Service should be involved in hearings on development proposals affecting the related sites. "Before, we'd have to read through the newspaper and see if any projects threatened to impact the park," says Church. "Now, we're right there at the preliminary meetings."

With the county's full support, park officials now propose modifications to development projects that threaten the park's integrity. At one residential development, the county endorsed the park's request for a 75-foot wooded buffer between the homes and the park boundary. At another, outside television antennas and satellite dishes were prohibited. Developers now routinely impose deed restrictions that require earth-tone paints on house exteriors or landscaping that conceals homes.

Not every developer is so far-sighted. At an intersection leading to the Wilderness battlefield, a developer refused to comply with the county and the park's request to reduce the size of a sign in front of a fast-food restaurant. (The county has a weak sign-control ordinance.) "We're about to have an 18-foot-high sign near the gateway to the battlefield," says Church. In most cases, however, the park's needs are met without compromising the landowner's expectations.

Park officials also have cultivated local organizations. Together with the Historic Fredericksburg Foundation and the Association for the Protection of Civil War Sites, the park hosted a series of informational seminars to brief elected officials on planning and design techniques for preserving battlefields and historic buildings. Park rangers also attend neighborhood association meetings to show homeowners how they can protect the battlefields' integrity. The Park Service's national office has helped, too, funneling $30,000 in grants to local planning and conservation programs and helping the county prepare design standards for lands adjacent to battlefield sites.

"Park officials have made it a priority to establish good relations with the community," says Catherine Gilliam, former director of the Historic Fredericksburg Foundation. "The payoff is that they've been able to realize their mission far better than if they had simply thrown their weight around."

## Notes

**page 49**: For more information on the value of dialogue and visioning, see *Community and the Politics of Place: Develop a Widely Shared Vision*, 1990, by Daniel Kemmis, University of Oklahoma Press, Norman, Oklahoma.

**page 51**: For more information on Lander's success with visioning, contact the Lander Chamber of Commerce, 160 N. First, Lander, Wyoming 82520, phone: (307) 332-3892.

**page 52**: For details about Chattanooga's visioning process, contact River-Valley Partners, 835 Georgia Avenue, Suite 500, Chattanooga, Tennessee 37402, phone: (423) 265-3700.

page 53: Information on the San Rafael Valley's vision for the future can be obtained from the San Rafael Valley Land Trust, HCR 2, Box 179, Patagonia, Arizona 85624, phone: (520) 455-5310. Also, see *A Framework for Guiding the Future of Arizona's San Rafael Valley*, 1994, by the San Rafael Valley Association and the Sonoran Institute, Tucson, Arizona.

page 54: For more information on Jackson Hole's visioning exercise and land-use plan, contact the Teton County Planning Department, P.O. Box 1727, Jackson, Wyoming 83001, phone: (307) 733-3959; or the Jackson Hole Alliance for Responsible Planning, P.O. Box 2728, Jackson, Wyoming 83001, phone: (307) 733-9417. The data on housing costs in Jackson are from *A Community Profile of Jackson Hole, Wyoming*, 1994. Jackson Hole Chamber of Commerce, Jackson, Wyoming.

page 54: For information on Jackson Hole's wildlife, see *Wildlife Winter Ranges on Private and Public Lands in Jackson Hole, Wyoming*, 1992. Biota Research and Consulting, Jackson, Wyoming; *Assessment of Habitat of Wildlife Communities of the Snake River, Jackson, Wyoming*, 1992, by R. L. Schroeder and A. W. Allen, U.S. Fish and Wildlife Service Research Publication 190; *Rare, Sensitive, and Threatened Species of the Greater Yellowstone Ecosystem*, 1989, edited by T. W. Clark, A. H. Harvey, R. D. Dorn, D. L. Genter, and C. Groves, published by the Northern Rockies Conservation Cooperative, Montana Natural Heritage Program, The Nature Conservancy –Idaho, Montana, and Wyoming field offices—and Mountain West Environmental Services. Also, contact the National Elk Refuge, 675 E. Broadway, Box C, Jackson, Wyoming 83001, phone: (307) 733-9212.

### Create an Inventory of Local Resources

page 59: For more information about growth pressures in eastern Tennessee, contact the Foothills Land Conservancy, 352 High Street, Maryville, Tennessee 37804, phone: (615) 681-8326.

page 60: Details about the performance-based development code in Breckenridge, Colorado, are available from the Breckenridge Planning Department, P.O. Box 168, Breckenridge, Colorado 80424, phone: (970) 453-3160.

page 60: For more information about Sanibel Island, contact Sanibel Department of Natural Resources, 800 Dunlop Road, Sanibel, Florida 33957, phone: (941) 472-3700; Sanibel Department of Planning, 800 Dunlop Road, Sanibel, Florida 33957, phone: (941) 472-4136; J.N. "Ding" Darling National Wildlife Refuge, One Wildlife Drive, Sanibel, Florida 33957, phone: (941) 472-1100; Sanibel–Captiva Conservation Foundation, P.O. Box 839, Sanibel, Florida 33957, phone: (941) 472-2329. See also *The Sanibel Report: Formulation of a Comprehensive Plan Based on Natural Systems*, 1976, by John Clark, The Conservation Foundation, Washington, D.C.

## Build on Local Assets

**page 64:** For more information on Jackson's efforts to protect Wildcat Brook, contact the Jackson Town Hall at (603) 383-4223.

**page 65:** Details about Manteo's economic development program can be obtained from the Manteo Planning Department, P.O. Box 246, Manteo, North Carolina 27954, phone: (919) 473-2133.

**page 65:** For more information on Wyoming's Watchable Wildlife program, see *Selling Watchable Wildlife in a Sporting State*, 1994, by Walt Gasson and Larry L. Kruckenberg, a paper presented at the National Wildlife Diversity Conference, St. Louis, Missouri. Or contact the Wyoming Game and Fish Department, Information and Education Division, 5400 Bishop Boulevard, Cheyenne, Wyoming 82006, phone: (307) 777-4541.

**page 66:** Details of the trail system in Front Royal, Virginia, can be obtained from the Front Royal Chamber of Commerce, P.O. Box 568, Front Royal, Virginia 22630, phone: (540) 635-3185.

**page 67:** For information on Butte's economic revitalization program, contact the Butte Historic Preservation Department, 115 W. Granite, Butte, Montana 59701, phone: (406) 723-8262.

**page 67:** Information on Lowell is available from the Lowell Division of Planning and Development, 50 Arcand Drive, Lowell, Massachusetts 01852, phone: (508) 970-4270; or the Lowell National Historical Park, 222 Merrimack Street, Lowell, Massachusetts 01852, phone: (508) 459-1088.

**page 68:** For more about Dubois, Wyoming, contact the Dubois Chamber of Commerce, P.O. Box 632, Dubois, Wyoming 82513, phone: (307) 455-2556; or the National Bighorn Sheep Interpretive Center, P.O. Box 1435, Dubois, Wyoming 82513, phone: (307) 455-3429.

## Minimize the Need for Regulations

**page 72:** For details about Fredericksburg's tax-incentive program, contact the Fredericksburg Department of Planning and Community Development, 715 Princess Anne Street, Fredericksburg, Virginia 22401, phone: (540) 372-1179.

**page 72:** For more information about the Kenai River, contact The Nature Conservancy, Alaska Field Office, 421 W. First Avenue, Suite 200, Anchorage, Alaska 99501, phone: (907) 276-3133. See also *The Kenai River: A River at Risk*, 1995, published by the Kenai River King Salmon Fund, 34824 Kalifornsky Beach Road, Soldotna, Alaska 99669, phone: (907) 262-2492; and *A Framework for Guiding the Future of Alaska's Kenai River Watershed*, 1996, by the Kenai River Watershed Forum Steering Committee, Borough of Kenai Peninsula, Alaska, phone: (907) 262-6377.

**page 73:** Information about Lowell's low-interest-loan pool for restoring historic buildings is available from the Lowell Division of Planning and Development, 50 Arcand Drive, Lowell, Massachusetts 01852, phone: (508) 970-4270.

**page 74:** The Vermont Housing and Conservation Board can be reached at 136 1/2 Main Street, Montpelier, Vermont 05602, phone: (802) 828-3250.

**page 75:** The Monroe County Land Authority is at 3706 N. Roosevelt Boulevard, Suite I, Key West, Florida 33040, phone: (305) 292-4414.

**page 76:** The Sonoma County Agricultural Preservation and Open Space District is at 415 Russell Avenue, Santa Rosa, California 95403, phone: (707) 524-7360.

**page 76:** Information on Vail and Crested Butte's open-space programs is available from the Town of Vail, 75 S. Frontage Road, Vail, Colorado 81657, phone: (970) 479-2107, and the Town of Crested Butte, P.O. Box 39, Crested Butte, Colorado 81224, phone: (970) 349-5338.

**page 77:** For information on Missoula's open-space bond act, contact the Missoula Office of Community Development, 435 Ryman, Missoula, Montana 59802, phone: (406) 523-4669.

**page 77:** For more information on Boulder's open-space program, see the case study in chapter 2, or contact the Boulder Open Space Department, P.O. Box 791, Boulder, Colorado 80306, phone: (303) 441-3440.

**page 77:** For information on the easement donation program on Cape Cod, contact the Compact of Cape Cod Conservation Trusts, 3179 Main Street, P.O. Box 7, Barnstable, Massachusetts 02630, phone: (508) 362-9131.

**page 78:** The Aspen Valley Land Trust can be reached at P.O. Box 940, Aspen, Colorado 81612, phone: (970) 920-3806.

**page 78:** The Sigurd Olson Environmental Institute is at Northland College, Ashland, Wisconsin 54806, phone: (715) 682-1223.

**page 78:** The Foothills Land Conservancy is at 352 High Street, Maryville, Tennessee 37804, phone: (615) 681-8326.

**page 79:** The information on conservation easements was drawn, in part, from *Conservation Options: A Landowner's Guide*, 1993, by the Land Trust Alliance, 1319 F Street, N.W., Suite 501, Washington, D.C. 20004, phone: (202) 638-4725; and from *The Conservation Easement Handbook: Managing Land Conservation and Historic Preservation Easements*, 1988, by Janet Diehl and Thomas S. Barrett, published by the Trust for Public Land and the Land Trust Alliance and available from the Land Trust Alliance.

**page 79:** For more information on Calvert County's transfer of development rights program, contact the Calvert County Administration and Finance Department, Courthouse, 175 Main Street, Prince Frederick, Maryland 20678, phone: (301) 535-1600. See also *Managing Maryland's Growth: Transferable De-*

*velopment Rights*, 1995, Maryland Office of Planning, Baltimore, Maryland; and *Putting Transfer of Development Rights to Work in California*, 1993, by Rick Pruetz, Solano Press Books, Point Arena, California.

### Meet the Needs of Both Landowner and Community

**page 84:** For more information about voluntary impact fees in St. George, contact the Virgin River Land Preservation Association, P.O. Box 1804, St. George, Utah 84771, phone: (801) 674-1074. Rick Sant is quoted in the *Saint George Spectrum*.

**page 85:** For information about the Wal-Mart in Bennington, contact the Town of Bennington, 205 South Street, Bennington, Vermont 05201, phone: (802) 442-1037. For details on how a Wal-Mart can affect a community's business district, see Vermont Environmental Board, *St. Albans Group and Wal-Mart Stores, Inc.*, June 27, 1995, Application #6F0471-EB, 10 V.S.A. chapter 151.

**page 85:** For information about the Cannon Beach's ban on franchises, contact the City of Cannon Beach, P.O. Box 368, Cannon Beach, Oregon 97110, phone: (503) 436-2045.

**page 85:** For more information on the cluster and open-space zoning in Marine on St. Croix, contact the City of Marine on St. Croix, Box 234, Marine on St. Croix, Minnesota 55047, phone: (612) 433-3636.

**page 86:** Details about Martin County's impact fees can be obtained from the Martin County Building and Zoning Department, 2401 S.E. Monterey Road, Stuart, Florida 34996, phone: (407) 288-5501.

**page 87:** For information on the building-permit moratorium in Park County, Wyoming, contact the Park County Planning and Zoning Office, 1002 Sheridan Avenue, Cody, Wyoming 82414, phone: (307) 587-2204.

**page 89:** For details on the fiscal cost of residential development on Mount Desert Island, see *The Cumulative Impact of Development on Mount Desert Island, Maine*, 1988, Mount Desert Island League of Women Voters, P.O. Box 625, Southwest Harbor, Maine 04679, phone: (207) 244-5486.

**page 89:** For more information about balancing conservation and development in Tucson, contact the Rincon Institute, 7290 E. Broadway Boulevard, Suite M, Tucson, Arizona 85710, phone: (520) 290-0828; or Saguaro National Park, 3693 Old Spanish Trail, Tucson, Arizona 85730, phone: (520) 296-8576. For more information about environmentally responsible and master-planned communities, see "Building Community," by John T. Martin, *Urban Land*, March 1996, vol. 55, no. 3; "A Better Way to Build," by George Burton Brewster, *Urban Land*, June 1995, vol. 54, no. 6; and "A Revolution in the Business of Conservation," by Curtis J. Badger, *Urban Land*, June 1995, vol. 54, no. 6.

## Team Up with Public-Land Managers

**page 93:** Information on the conservation easement program at the San Luis National Wildlife Refuge is available from the San Luis National Wildlife Refuge Complex, P.O. Box 2176, Los Banos, California 93635, phone: (209) 826-3508.

**page 94:** For more information about land use adjacent to Cuyahoga Valley National Recreation Area, contact the Cuyahoga Valley Communities Council, 3 Brecksville Commons, Suite One, 8221 Brecksville Road, Brecksville, Ohio 44141, phone: (216) 526-1822; or the Cuyahoga Valley National Recreation Area, 15610 Vaughn Road, Brecksville, Ohio 44141, phone: (216) 526-5256.

**page 94:** For details about the Park Service's battlefield grants program, contact the American Battlefield Protection Program, National Park Service, 800 North Capitol Street, N.W., Suite 250, Washington, D.C. 20002, phone: (202) 343-9505

**page 95:** For more information on local land-acquisition programs on Cape Cod, contact the Compact of Cape Cod Conservation Trusts, 3179 Main Street, P.O. Box 7, Barnstable, Massachusetts 02630, phone: (508) 362-9131.

**pages 96–98:** Thanks to Gil Lusk for insights into tips for helping park and refuge managers build partnerships with communities.

**page 98:** For more information about Moab, contact the Canyon Country Partnership, P.O. Box 970, Moab, Utah 84532, phone: (801) 259-8372. See also "A Passive Utah Town Awaits Its Fate," by Florence Williams, *High Country News*, November 18, 1991, vol. 23, no. 21. The Edward Abbey quote is from *Desert Solitaire*, 1968, Ballantine Books, New York.

**page 101.** For more information about Estes Park, contact Estes Park Community Development Department, P.O. Box 1200, Estes Park, Colorado 80517, phone: (970) 586-5331; Larimer County Parks, Open Space Department, 1800 S. County Road 31, Loveland, Colorado 80537, phone: (970) 679-4570; and Rocky Mountain National Park, Estes Park, Colorado 80517, phone: (970) 586-1399.

**page 105:** For more information on Mount Desert Island, contact Acadia National Park, P.O. Box 177, Bar Harbor, Maine 04609, phone: (207) 288-3338; Friends of Acadia, P.O. Box 725, Bar Harbor, Maine 04609, phone: (207) 288-3340; and Maine Coast Heritage Trust, P.O. Box 426, Northeast Harbor, Maine 04662, phone: (207) 276-5156.

## Recognize the Role of Nongovernmental Organizations

The nongovernmental organizations mentioned in this chapter are happy to provide additional information about their results and programs.

pages 109–113: The International Sonoran Desert Alliance is at P.O. Box 687, Ajo, Arizona 85321, phone: (520) 387-6823. The Tyrrell County Community Development Corporation is at P.O. Box 58, Columbia, North Carolina 27925, phone: (919) 796-0193. The Marin Agricultural Land Trust is at P.O. Box 809, Point Reyes Station, California 94956, phone: (415) 663-1158. The Willapa Alliance is at P.O. Box 278, South Bend, Washington 98586, phone: (360) 875-5195. The Teton Valley Economic Development Council is at P.O. Box 756, Driggs, Idaho 83422, phone: (208) 354-2593. The Mesa County Land Conservancy is at 2600 N. 12th Street, Grand Junction, Colorado 81501, phone: (970) 241-2832. The Champlain Valley Heritage Network is at Route 1, Box 220, Crown Point, New York 12928, phone: (518) 597-4646. The Malpai Borderlands Group can be reached at P.O. Box Drawer 3536, Douglas, Arizona 85608, phone: (520) 558-2470.

page 113: For more information about Red Lodge, contact the Beartooth Front Community Forum, P.O. Box 454, Red Lodge, Montana 59068, phone: (406) 446-3843. Housing and rental cost figures are from the *City of Red Lodge Housing Plan*, 1993, by Double-Tree, Inc.; and *Final Environmental Impact Statement for the Red Lodge Mountain Ski Area Master Development Plan*, 1996. USDA Forest Service, Custer National Forest, Beartooth Ranger District, Red Lodge, Montana.

### *Provide Opportunities for Leaders to Step Forward*

pages 120 and 121: For more information about Betty Rankin, Annie Snyder, or Larry Mann, see *Rally Behind the Virginians*, 1994, a video produced by Grunwald, Eskew, Donilon, Washington, D.C.

page 120: For more information on Tom Huerkamp, see "Colorado's Prison Slayer: One Man's Quest to Unshackle a Rural Economy," by Paul Larmer, *High Country News*, June 26, 1995, vol. 27, no. 25.

page 124: For more information on Penn Center and the Sea Islands, contact Penn Center, P.O. Box 126, St. Helena Island, South Carolina 29920, phone: (803) 838-2432. The figures on water use on Hilton Head Island are from "Islands under Siege," by David S. Broder, *The Washington Post*, August 16, 1989.

### *Pay Attention to Aesthetics*

page 126: For information about visual amenities and market prices, see *Value by Design: Landscape, Site Planning, and Amenities*, 1994, by Lloyd W. Bookout, Michael D. Beyard, and Steven W. Fader. The Urban Land Institute, Washington, D.C.

**page 126**: For more information about Lander, contact the Lander Chamber of Commerce, 160 N. First, Lander, Wyoming 82520, phone: (307) 332-3892.

**page 127**: For details on Coral Gables's design incentives, contact the Coral Gables Planning Department, P.O. Drawer 141549, Coral Gables, Florida 33114, phone: (305) 460-5214.

**page 130**: For more information about Fredericksburg, contact the Fredericksburg Department of Planning and Community Development, 715 Princess Anne Street, Fredericksburg, Virginia 22401, phone: (540) 372-1179; Fredericksburg and Spotsylvania National Military Park, 120 Chatham Lane, Fredericksburg, Virginia 22401, phone: (540) 371-0802; or the Historic Fredericksburg Foundation, P.O. Box 8327, Fredericksburg, Virginia 22404, phone: (540) 371-4504.

# Chapter 5

## Conclusion

An increasing number of Americans are choosing to live next to national parks, national wildlife refuges, and other public lands and natural areas. For the communities around them, the result is change, often at an unprecedented pace.

Yet change need not come at the expense of local values. A growing and convincing body of evidence demonstrates that communities can in fact manage growth and development so that they enhance rather than detract from local values and quality of life. Each of the communities profiled in this book is taking steps to see that development meets local aspirations, contributes to a healthy economy, and respects the natural and cultural values of the surrounding landscape.

While local approaches for integrating conservation and development must be tailored to the unique circumstances facing each community, our travels and research indicate that successful local initiatives tend to share several factors. In other words, success doesn't happen by chance. Results can never be guaranteed, but there are several guidelines that can help a community achieve them. To recap our findings:

Public involvement and participation are integral elements of nearly every successful initiative profiled in these pages. Communities need to continuously involve their citizens in any program to determine future land-use or economic development patterns. Engaging citizens in "envisioning" the future of the community may be a never-ending process, but it can pay off handsomely: In Chattanooga, Tennessee, for example, a participatory visioning process was the foundation of a successful effort to revitalize the entire city. While a commitment to meaningful public participation does not ensure success, it is rare indeed to find a successful local strategy that has been built on half-hearted or *pro forma* public participation.

Meaningful citizen participation also requires a concerted effort to bring *all* interest groups and perspectives to the table. Too often, local initiatives rely on elaborate efforts to involve only those whose perspectives are comfortable to the county commissioners, city council, or nonprofit organization organizing the local dialogue process. This recommendation isn't based on altruism or an abstract commitment to democracy: Ironically, the torpedo that most often sinks a promising effort is not disagreement over goals or strategies but the resistance that comes from people who feel left out of a process or who believe—fairly or unfairly—that an effort was "planned on" them rather than with them.

Citizens also have to be involved as leaders as well as participants. Inviting citizens to an announcement of a decision or to a public hearing on a narrow issue does not qualify as public involvement. Local people must become actively involved in both determining the future direction of the community and in carrying out specific programs to realize that vision. If you're still skeptical, take another look at Red Lodge, Montana.

Another lesson is that communities need to make sure that they have the information necessary to make sound decisions. At the same time, a community should not allow a lack of "adequate data" to paralyze action. While a locality needs to make decisions based on the best available information, bear in mind that governing requires judgment and that "adequate data" is no substitute for that judgment. We advise local decision makers to collect the best available information and then to take action that allows for future adaptations based on new information and changing circumstances.

Perhaps communities should heed the advice of Colin Powell, former chairman of the Joint Chiefs of Staff, who has said the window of opportunity for action occurs when decision makers possess between 40 and 70 percent of the information they need. Having less information is acting in the dark, he maintains, while waiting for more can foreclose opportunities for results.

A community also should fashion local initiatives around its distinctive assets, the features that set it apart from other communities and make it unique. In most cases, economic development strategies that accentuate a community's distinctive assets should be embraced. At the same time, a community should make certain that its most special attributes are not damaged or excessively commercialized. In a rapidly globalizing economy, a community that preserves its distinctive assets preserves its economic future. In Jackson, New Hampshire, the distinctive asset was a waterfall. In Sanibel, Florida, it was unbroken stretches of beach and healthy populations of fish and wildlife.

This observation may be of little use to the many American communities that have already been homogenized by franchise architecture, strip development, or cookie-cutter design standards. But it still applies to many rural communities where residents may be overlooking their rich natural or cultural assets. Examples here include the bighorn sheep herd of Dubois, Wyoming; the Revolutionary War history of Schuylerville, New York; and the industrial heritage of Lowell, Massachusetts—all of which were only recently recognized as important community assets.

All communities, of course, rely to some extent on regulations to protect local values and promote desired characteristics in new development. In a complex, crowded world, regulations are essential for providing a minimum code of conduct. At the same time, we've discovered that communities often depend too heavily on them. Regulations may be effective at preventing the worst in new development, but by themselves they cannot bring out the best. Overreliance on regulatory approaches—without equal or greater emphasis on more *innovative* and *inclusive* approaches—can be counterproductive.

In some communities, innovation simply means using native vegetation on public lawns as a precedent to enacting a local ordinance mandating such landscaping. In others, it means an awards program recognizing excellence in design or celebrating a business that exceeds emissions standards. It may also mean establishing a local low-interest loan fund to promote sustainable businesses or to finance historic preservation. In Fredericksburg, Virginia, tax incentives spurred renovation of historic buildings; in Staunton, Virginia, free design assistance achieved the same goal. Regulations were only a small part of each city's program. Public education campaigns are almost always an element of effective initiatives.

In addition, an increasing number of communities—and not just big cities and wealthy suburbs, but rural communities that already contain substantial amounts of public land—have complemented regulatory programs with public acquisition of critical lands or the acquisition of agricultural preservation easements on surrounding lands.

Another of our findings is that successful communities have transcended the "growth versus no-growth" wars that characterize land-use policy in many cities and towns. Instead of opposing every new development, or approving it willy-nilly, communities need to work upfront with developers to achieve a desirable mix of uses.

We all are familiar with the highly regulated, wealthy enclaves that allow only the most desirable uses of land and then only after the most intense scrutiny. But we also should recognize that these communities simply export or externalize the less desirable, less manicured land uses to other communities.

By our standards, gateway communities should offer housing not only to wealthy retirees and visitors but also to the workforce that makes the community hum. In our view, if there is not enough room for affordable housing, then the community probably has an imbalance between the amount of land dedicated to commercial development and the amount available for housing. Jackson, Wyoming, and Mount Desert Island, Maine, for example, are making it a priority to increase the amount of affordable housing available for residents earning a median income.

Development should not only be fiscally sound, environmentally responsible, and aesthetically pleasing, it also must create a balanced, livable community. In almost every gateway community we visited, a broad cross-section of residents expressed strong support for a diverse community with a balanced, multifaceted economy. To achieve this, communities need to consciously maintain a balance of various land uses—commercial and residential, large lot and small lot, farmland and industrial. This requires that they not simply export problematic land uses, but that they work closely with landowners and developers upfront to make sure that development meets local aspirations.

By nature, a gateway community adjoins public lands or protected areas. Many gateway communities unfortunately have gotten sidetracked by the hot-headed rhetoric that often envelops public-land management agencies. On the one hand are local leaders who describe public agencies as unfeeling bureaucracies bent on squeezing local towns into oblivion, curtailing access to public land, or destroying local customs and culture. On the other are those who say public agencies work mindlessly to increase the number of tourists to an area or to subsidize extractive industries at the expense of other values and enterprises.

This rhetoric often creates a one-dimensional view of what are in fact complex organizations. To be sure, we've run into individual public-land managers who personify either extreme. But we've also seen that successful initiatives often are launched only when local leaders and public-land managers look beyond the rhetoric and strive for solutions that promote the priorities of both the community *and* the public agency. As this book catalogs, more and more landowners, local governments, and public-land managers are living up to this challenge.

Finally, any community interested in becoming balanced and livable should seek out and actively solicit partners: citizens groups; local, regional, or national nonprofit organizations; business associations; neighboring towns; and philanthropic foundations. The challenges facing today's communities demand a great deal of expertise and sophistication; it's unlikely that a community will achieve results without assistance from others. Gateway communities have an edge over most communities, however, in that they have a nearby public agency that's usually more than willing to be a partner.

Make no mistake, the solutions and lessons we've outlined in this book take plenty of time and plenty of effort. Success is never guaranteed, and every setting requires an individually tailored approach. Moreover, initiatives must go forward in the face of many uncertainties and with the need to readily adapt to changing circumstances.

Community-based approaches and partnerships between gateway communities and neighboring public agencies won't always ensure an outcome that realizes local aspirations and respects natural and cultural assets. Without these approaches, though, we will surely fail in our efforts to protect both our most cherished landscapes and the integrity of the communities that adjoin them.

# Suggestions for Further Reading

## Community Inventories

*Where We Live: A Citizen's Guide to Conducting a Community Environmental Inventory*, by Donald F. Harker and Elizabeth Ungar Natter. 1995. Island Press, Washington, D.C.

A primer on the indicators needed to undertake an inventory of local trends and conditions.

*Regional Economic Information System*, Bureau of Economic Analysis (BE-55), U.S. Department of Commerce. 1996. Washington, D.C. 20230. Phone: (202) 606-5360.

Comprehensive data on employment and income trends for every U.S. county. CD-ROM data available for $35 and contains complete state and county economic data from 1969 to 1991. Data also available in diskette or print-out.

*County Business Patterns*, Bureau of the Census, U.S. Department of Commerce, Washington, D.C. 20233. Phone: (202) 763-4100.

County and state information on wages and business establishments. CD-ROM data available for $150 and contains complete state and county economic data.

## Community Planning

*A Concise Guide to Community Planning*, by Kenneth B. Hall Jr. and Gerald A. Porterfield. 1995. McGraw-Hill, New York City.

A handbook to help communities plan for their future.

*Community and the Politics of Place,* by Daniel Kemmis. 1990. University of
   Oklahoma Press, Norman, Oklahoma.
An eloquent call to involve citizens in planning for the future of their communities.


## Conservation Easements

*The Conservation Easement Handbook: Managing Land Conservation and
   Historic Preservation Easement Programs,* by Janet Diehl and Thomas S.
   Barrett. 1988. The Trust for Public Land and the Land Trust Alliance,
   Alexandria, Virginia.
Quite simply, the bible on conservation easements.

*Preserving Family Lands: Essential Tax Strategies for the Landowner,* by Stephen Small. 1993. Landowner Planning Center, Boston.
A how-to guide to the tax code for families and landowners who care about the future of their land.


## Design

*Guiding Principles of Sustainable Design.* 1993. National Park Service, Denver.
A complete guide to all the principles of sustainable design: landscaping, water and
energy conservation, building design, and site planning.

*Saving Face: How Corporate Franchise Design Can Respect Community Iden-
   tity,* by Ronald Fleming. 1994. American Planning Association, Chicago.
A comprehensive look at how communities can ensure franchise designs respect
local character.

*Rural by Design,* by Randall Arendt. 1994. American Planning Association,
   Chicago.
A how-to manual filled with case studies and techniques to help small towns and
rural communities retain their character.

*Value by Design: Landscape, Site Planning, and Amenities,* by Lloyd W. Bookout, Michael D. Beyard, and Steven W. Fader. 1994. Washington, D.C.
   The Urban Land Institute.
An analysis of how attractive landscaping and design add value to real estate ven-
tures.

*Sign Regulation for Small and Midsize Communities,* by E. D. Kelly and Gary
   Raso. 1989. American Planning Association, Chicago.
How a community can control the design, location, and size of signs.

## Economics

*Job Creation in America: How the Smallest Companies Put the Most People to Work*, by David Birch. 1987. Free Press, New York.

An investigation of the sources of job growth in today's economy.

*The Work of Nations: Preparing Ourselves for 21st Century Capitalism*, by Robert B. Reich. 1991. Alfred A. Knopf, New York.

A look at global economic trends and how governments and communities can prepare for them.

*The Economic Impacts of Protecting Rivers, Trails, and Greenway Corridors.* 1994. National Park Service, Washington, D.C.

A compilation of information documenting the positive economic impact of trails and greenways.

*Paying for Growth, Prospering from Development*, by Michael Kinsley. 1995. Rocky Mountain Institute, Snowmass, Colorado.

An examination of the fiscal costs of growth and development.

*Measuring Change in Rural Economies: A Workbook for Determining Demographic, Economic, and Fiscal Trends*, by Ray Rasker, Jerry Johnson, and Vicky York. 1994. The Wilderness Society and Bolle Center for Ecosystem Management, Washington, D.C.

A workbook to help determine a community or region's economic picture.

## Grants

*Directory to Environmental Grantmaking Foundations*, by the Environmental Data Research Institute. Published annually.

A complete guide to more than 600 corporate, private, and community foundations.

## Growth Management and Land-Use Planning

*Creating Successful Communities: A Guidebook to Growth Management Strategies*, by Michael Mantell, Stephen Harper, and Luther Propst—The Conservation Foundation. 1989. Island Press, Washington, D.C.

A comprehensive guide—including numerous examples and case studies—to local land-use planning and conservation tools.

*Managing Development in Small Towns*, by David J. Brower, C. Carraway, T. Pollard, and Luther Propst. 1984. Planner's Press, Washington, D.C.

An extensive look at the tools and techniques that small towns can use to manage growth.

## Historic Preservation

*Innovative Tools for Historic Preservation*, by Marya Morris. 1992. American
   Planning Association, Chicago.

A complete guide to historic preservation techniques, including preservation districts, zoning, and tax and financial incentives.

## Market Approaches

*Our Lands: New Strategies for Protecting the West*, by the Western Governors'
   Association. 1993.

Twelve case studies highlighting market-based and cooperative approaches to resource management and planning, including negotiating win-win settlements, creating better pricing signals, offering incentives, and encouraging voluntary initiatives.

## Organizational Resources

*Starting a Land Trust: A Guide to Forming a Land Conservation Organization*,
   by the Land Trust Alliance. 1990. Washington, D.C.

Required reading for anyone interested in creating their own nonprofit organization. Includes information on incorporating, maintaining tax-exempt status, selecting a board of directors, and raising funds.

*Tax-Exempt Status for Your Organization* (Publication 557), the Internal
   Revenue Service. Available free from any IRS clearinghouse.

This 40-page pamphlet explains the legal and tax issues involved with creating a new organization.

## Tourism

*Nature Tourism: Managing for the Environment*, edited by Tensie Whelan.
   1993. Island Press, Washington, D.C.

A practical manual for communities interested in developing a nature tourism industry.

*Getting Started: How to Succeed in Heritage Tourism*, by the National Trust
   for Historic Preservation. 1993. Washington, D.C.

How a community can preserve and benefit from its history. Available in both book and video.

### Trails, Rivers, and Greenways

*Greenways: A Guide to Planning, Design and Development*, edited by Loring LaB. Schwarz—The Conservation Fund. 1993. Island Press, Washington, D.C.

This how-to manual provides citizens and community officials with the tools to plan and develop a greenway.

*Trails for the 21st Century: Planning, Design, and Management Manual for Multi-Use Trails*, edited by Karen-Lee Ryan. 1993. Island Press, Washington, D.C.

A practical guide to creating and managing multiple-use trails.

*How to Save a River: A Handbook for Citizen Action*, by David Bolling. 1995. Island Press, Washington, D.C.

A complete guide to river conservation, including tips on how to organize citizens, plan a campaign, and develop alternatives to water projects.

### Transportation

*At Road's End: Transportation and Land-Use Choices for Communities*, by Daniel Carlson with Lisa Wormser and Cy Ulberg. 1995. Island Press, Washington, D.C.

Ways to integrate bike paths and pedestrian walkways into a community's transportation system.

# Index